History Upside Down

History Upside Down

The Roots of Palestinian Fascism and the Myth of Israeli Aggression

DAVID MEIR-LEVI

A David Horowitz Freedom Center Book

BRIEF ENCOUNTERS

Encounter Books · New York · London

Copyright © 2007 by David Meir-Levi

First edition published in 2007 by Encounter Books, an activity of Encounter for Culture and Education, Inc., a nonprofit, tax exempt corporation.

Encounter Books website address: *www.encounterbooks.com*

Manufactured in the United States and printed on acid-free paper. The paper used in this publication meets the minimum requirements of ANSI/NISO Z39.48–1992 (R 1997) (Permanence of Paper).

FIRST EDITION

LIBRARY OF CONGRESS CATALOGING-IN-PUBLICATION DATA

Meir-Levi, David.
History upside down : the roots of Palestinian fascism and the myth of Israeli aggression / by David Meir-Levi.
p.   cm.
ISBN-13: 978-1-59403-192-2 (hardcover : alk. paper)
ISBN-10: 1-59403-192-4 (hardcover : alk. paper)
1. Arab-Israeli conflict.   2. National liberation movements—Palestine.
3. Nationalism—Palestine.   4. Jihad.   5. Islam and politics—Palestine.
6. Zionism—Palestine.   I. Title.
DS119.7.M4322 2007
956.95´3044—dc22
2007031290

10 9 8 7 6 5 4 3 2 1

Contents

Introduction

THE BASIC SCRIPT of the Middle East conflict has changed over the last generation, and the version in which it has come to present itself has profoundly distorted the meaning of events and obscured this regional conflict's role in the general war that Islamic radicals have declared against the West.

On its creation by the United Nations in 1948, the state of Israel was attacked by five Muslim Arab nations whose goal, in the words of Hassan al-Banna, founder of the Muslim Brotherhood, was "to push the Jews into the sea." Although outnumbered, the Israelis prevailed. But the Arab states refused to sign a peace, or to create the state that the United Nations had reserved for the Arab population on the west bank of the Jordan and in Gaza. This Arab war against the existence of the Jewish state has been waged for sixty years without let-up.

In 1967, a second aggression by the Arab states, led by the Egyptian dictator Gamal Abdel Nasser, ended with Israel occupying the West Bank and Gaza—the corridors through which the Arab armies had designed their attack. The Israelis were unable to withdraw their forces and maintain their security because their Arab enemies continued refusing to recognize the legitimacy of the Israeli state and to sign a permanent peace agreement.

Introduction

Until that victory in 1967, the Israeli democracy had been widely seen as the David of the Middle East, menaced by the totalitarian Goliaths of the surrounding Arab states, who wished it dead. But beginning with the Six-Day War and with growing force since then, that perception has changed. Attention has shifted from the aggressors (Egypt, Syria, Jordan, Saudi Arabia, and Iraq) to the Arabs living in the West Bank and Gaza, who began calling themselves "Palestinians" at about the same time that they formed a "national liberation movement." Thus Israel became the Goliath, and the "Palestinians" were now David.

Under Yassir Arafat, this Palestinian movement packaged its cause so adroitly that today it is Israel that is seen as the threatening giant—a heartless occupying power that is colonialist and imperialist, squeezing the life out of a homeless people and denying their national aspirations. So successful has this campaign against Israel been that the Palestinians and their apologists, particularly in Europe, have successfully claimed that the Israelis, a people living in the shadow of the Holocaust, are themselves "Nazis." In demonstrations around the world, the Star of David is routinely shown as equaling the swastika; the faces of Ariel Sharon and other Israeli leaders are morphed into the image of Adolf Hitler.

This book rejects the arrant absurdity of such comparisons (particularly given the fact that every day brings more proof that Iran's Ahmadinejad, Hamas' Nasrallah, and other radical Muslims *all* yearn for a solution as final as the Nazis'); it also rejects the idea that the basic situation in the Middle East has changed since the United Nations established the Jewish state and the Palestinian state that would have stood alongside it, if not for Arab intransigence. The issue in the

Middle East is today what it has been since the Muslim invasion in the seventh century: the Arabs' hatred of the Jews. Jew-hatred goes back to the very beginnings of Islam. So too does genocide, as an end-of-days Armageddon scenario.

Apologists for the Arab world and Muslim culture routinely deny it, but testimony from Muslim refugees and the documentation in books and websites and video documentaries is overwhelming. An essential part of Arab education, from earliest childhood onward, is a dehumanizing hatred for the Jews as the enemies of Islam and of Allah. Jews are depicted as subhuman (based on Qur'an 5:60, for example, where Allah likens them to swine and apes) and at the same time as deviously intelligent, using their wiles and machinations for world domination and evil plots against Islam. Not only is everything Jewish evil, but everything evil is Jewish. Hence, as the ancient Hadith of the Tree and the Stone instructs believing Muslims, the Jews, all Jews worldwide, must be destroyed.

It has been but a short step from the religious principle to the political commitment. Part One of this book traces the development of Palestinian nationalism and shows how, building on the Muslim anti-Semitism that has existed in the Middle East for well over a thousand years, that nationalism found soul mates in Nazi fascism and Soviet communism— the one totalitarianism giving the Arab world's inchoate hatred of Jews a systematic intellectual structure; the other showing it how to cloak its genocidal intentions with the mantle of oppression. In helping shape the Palestinian movement, these totalitarian ideologies led directly to the Islamo-fascism of Hamas.

Instrumental in this grafting was the Grand Mufti of

Introduction

Jerusalem, Haj Amin al-Husseini, unchallenged spiritual leader of the Muslims of British Mandatory Palestine, who begged Hitler to exterminate European Jewry and then do the same to the Jews of Palestine.

But the Nazification of Muslim Jew-hatred continued long after the Third Reich was destroyed. Nazi refugees found haven and employment in Arab countries, where they helped craft the next generation of anti-Jewish and anti-Israel propaganda and educational curricula, all intended to teach the next generation of Muslims that there could be no treaty with Israel, no peace for the Jew.

Communism took Palestinian nationalism to the next step of its development during the Cold War. With the USSR as their ally, and Eastern bloc satellite countries as their haven and training ground, the dozens of Arab terrorist groups that burst out of the Middle East after the Six-Day War learned (some at Patrice Lumumba People's Friendship University in Moscow) to apply Communist techniques—chief among them posturing as a national liberation movement—to their unremitting terror war against Israel.

By depicting Israel to a credulous Western audience as the roadblock to peace, the final bastion of Western imperialism, the last and the worst of the oppressive Western occupiers of Third World countries, and a racist, apartheid, genocidal regime to boot, Arab propaganda under Communist tutelage transmuted unacceptable anti-Semitism into a justifiable anti-Zionism, and turned an odious Jew-hatred into a politically correct Israel-hatred. Israel thus was rendered the Jew among nations.

Hamas reconnected a Palestinian nationalism shaped by fascism and communism to its traditional Muslim sources

x

in creating an ideology that transformed the Arab-Israeli conflict from an argument about land into an eschatological conflict for which all treaties are irrelevant, all agreements are temporary, and the only acceptable resolution is a victory entailing nothing less than the utter destruction of Israel and the genocide of all the world's Jews. This heinous evil, in fact, is at the core of the Hamas Covenant.

The Palestinian movement for national self-determination, from Haj Amin to Arafat and from Fatah to Hamas, is the only one in world history for which terrorism is its sole defining paradigm, and which has as its unique and uncompromising goal the total destruction of a sovereign state and the genocide of its citizens.

Part One of this book brings into focus the political DNA whose strands make up the Palestinian movement. Part Two examines the cornerstone myths that this movement has created, largely for a Western audience, to serve as the seemingly rational basis for the irrational—and irrationally per-durable—terror war it has waged against Israel.

These myths seek to make the terrorism of the last decades not only rational, but heroic. Turning Middle East history upside down and inside out, they make the victim into the aggressor and the aggressor into the victim. Along the way, they legitimize the genocidal goals of the Arab terrorist parties.

One such myth is the notion that the Israelis stole the Palestinians' land in 1948 and ever since have blocked the creation of a motherland for the homeless Palestinians. But the sequence of events following the UN Security Council Resolution 181 in 1947 demonstrates beyond doubt that the

Introduction

failure to fulfill the world body's vision of two states, living side by side, cooperating economically and politically to mutual benefit, rests heavily on the Arab side. Israel accepted the partition plan and extended its hand to all Arab neighbors. Israel and a state for the Arabs, as envisioned by the UN, could have existed side by side with mutual benefit, had the Arab side been willing. The Arab side was not. The land set aside for a Palestinian state was annexed by Egypt and Jordan. It was the Arabs, not the Jews, who stole the Palestinians' land.

An even more inflammatory myth concerns the issue of the Arab refugees. Contrary to the successful propaganda campaign the Arab world has waged, the creation of Israel did not cause the refugee problem; nor was there ever a systematic attempt by Israeli forces to practice ethnic cleansing. The Arab leaders, including Haj Amin himself, urged and in some cases forced Arab peasantry to flee at the onset of the 1948 war with the intent that they would return after the inevitable Israeli defeat, when they would take back their land and also the land of the Jews.

Finally there is the myth of the "occupation" in the West Bank and the Gaza Strip, which the Arabs have claimed was the legacy of the 1967 war. The core of the Arab propaganda argument demonizing and delegitimizing the Israeli communities in these areas, and the Israeli government policies relating to them, is that they are illegal by international law, that they grab Arab land from helpless Arab peasants, and that they monopolize scarce water resources to the detriment of the Arab population. Every one of these assertions intentionally distorts the reality of the Israeli economic development of the West Bank and Gaza, obfuscates improvements in Arab quality of life that accrued thanks to Israel after the Six-Day War, and ignores the Israeli government's commitment to the legal purchase of privately owned Arab land or legally owned "crown land" for the construction and expansion of Israeli communities.

The endless charges about an "illegal occupation" and "land grab" constitute the most carefully crafted and effectively deployed strategy in the propaganda war that the Arab world has waged against Israel since the multiple failures of Arab armies and Arab terrorism to destroy the Jewish state.

In the new narrative cynically crafted over the past four decades by the Palestinians and their Communist and Islamist sponsors, the Middle East situation is on the one hand an isolated example of a tyrannical power oppressing a helpless and homeless people, and on the other the world's geopolitical wound whose healing is necessary to end the clash of civilizations between Islam and the West. The historical record shows that this is a convenient untruth and that the reality is much starker. Behind the war waged on Israel's southern front by Hamas is Iran. Behind the war waged against Israel's northern front by Hezbollah is also Iran. Behind the genocidal ideology of all three is the Muslim Brotherhood, inspiration for al-Qaeda and for the global Islamofascist crusade. Viewed in the accurate prism of the Islamic war against the West, Israel can be seen as a democracy on the frontline of the "war on terror," where it has been under siege since long before that phrase was conceived after 9/11.

PART ONE

1 | The Nazi Roots of Palestinian Nationalism and Islamic Jihad

ON OCTOBER 28, 2005, President George W. Bush used the term "Islamic fascism" to describe the Muslim terrorist groups currently at war with the West.[1] He denounced them as movements that have a "violent and political vision," and that call for "the establishment by terrorism, subversion and insurgency, of a totalitarian empire that denies all political and religious freedom."

Bush's remarks sparked an outburst of condemnation from the political left. Some of the very same Muslim movements to which the president referred, critics pointed out, were self-defined popular resistance movements that present themselves as seeking just and legitimate national self-determination for their oppressed people. How can such fighters, with all the cachet of rebels leading a just and honorable cause, be compared to the Nazis, who began a war that killed seventy million people and put the word "genocide" in the modern vocabulary?

But the president was right. The Muslim groups that today threaten the West with terrorism, subversion, and insurgency, and which seek, in their own words, to bring about a global totalitarian empire, not only are fascist in the broad sociological sense, but can trace their historical origins to the Nazi fascism of the Third Reich.

David Meir-Levi

FATAL ATTRACTION: THE MUSLIM
BROTHERHOOD AND THE NAZIS

The ideology of today's Islamists—Hamas and Hezbollah and also al-Qaeda itself—originated with Egypt's Muslim Brotherhood (*al-Ikhwan al-Muslimun*), founded in 1928 by Sheikh Hassan al-Banna (1906–1949).[2]

Al-Banna was born into the family of a poor watchmaker in southern Egypt. While still in his teens, he was attracted to the extremist and xenophobic aspects of an Islam that was hostile to Western secularism and its system of rights, particularly women's rights. The young al-Banna and his friends (they referred to each other as "brethren") met frequently to discuss the situation in the Middle East, to argue about the ills of Arab society, and to lament the decline of Islam. Their angst was in large part a reaction to the collapse of the Ottoman Empire, the British occupation of Egypt, and the resulting exposure of Arab society to Western values.

For al-Banna, as for many other Muslims worldwide, the end of the Muslim Caliphate, although brought about by secular Muslim Turks, was a sacrilege against Islam that could ultimately be blamed on the non-Muslim West. The desire to strike back against these evils led al-Banna to found the Muslim Brotherhood in 1928.

It began as a kind of youth club where the members preached, to anyone who would listen, about the need for moral reform in the Arab world. But al-Banna's antipathy toward Western modernity soon moved him to try to shape the Brotherhood into an organization that could check the secularist tendencies in Muslim society by asserting a return to ancient and traditional Islamic values. He recruited followers from a large cross-section of Egyptian society by addressing issues such as colonialism, public health, educational policy, natural resources management, social inequalities, Arab nationalism, the weakness of the Islamic world, and the growing conflict in Palestine. Among the perspectives he drew on to address these issues were the anticapitalist doctrines of European Marxism and especially fascism. The Nazis spoke the language of raw power and so did al-Banna: "It is the nature of Islam to dominate, not to be dominated, to impose its law on all nations, and to extend its power to the entire planet."

As the group expanded during the 1930s and broadened its activities well beyond its original religious revivalism, al-Banna began dreaming a greater Muslim dream: the restoration of the Caliphate, unifying the Muslim world in a global Islamic empire. He would describe, in inflammatory speeches, the horrors of hell expected for heretics, and consequently the need for Muslims to return to their purest religious roots and resume the great and final holy war, or jihad, against the non-Muslim world. And it was this dream, which al-Banna believed could become a reality only by the sword, that won the hearts and minds of a growing legion of followers.

Al-Banna's message resonated throughout the Arab world. By 1938, the Brotherhood's membership had grown to almost two hundred thousand, with fifty branches in Egypt alone. The organization established mosques, schools, sports clubs, factories, and a welfare service network. By the end of the 1930s, more than a half million active members were registered in more than two thousand branches across the Arab world. In British Mandatory Palestine alone there were thirty-eight branches.

To achieve that broader dream of a global jihad, the Brotherhood developed a network of underground cells, stole weapons, trained fighters, formed secret assassination squads, founded sleeper cells of supporters in the ranks of the army and the police, and waited for the order to go public with terrorism, assassinations, and suicide missions.[3]

It was during this time that the Muslim Brotherhood began a collaboration with Nazi Germany. Hitler's Reich offered al-Banna's movement great power connections and other advantages, but the relationship brokered by the Brotherhood was more than a diplomatic marriage of convenience. Long before the war, al-Banna had developed an Islamic religious ideology that in fact anticipated the Nazi ideology. Both movements sought world conquest and domination. Both were triumphalist and supremacist: in Nazism, the Aryan must rule, while in al-Banna's Islam, the Muslim religion must hold dominion. Both advocated subordination of the individual to a folkish central power. Both were explicitly antinationalist in the sense that they believed in the liquidation of the nation-state in favor of a transnational unifying community: in Islam, the *Umma* (community of all believers); and in Nazism, the *Herrenvolk* (master race). Both worshipped a unifying totalitarian figure, the caliph or the Führer. And both rabidly hated the Jews and sought their destruction.

As the Brotherhood entered a political and military relationship with Nazi Germany, these parallels facilitated practical interactions that created a full-blown alliance, with all the pomp and panoply of formal state visits, de facto ambassadors, and overt as well as *sub rosa* joint ventures. Al-Banna's followers easily transplanted into the receptive

Arab world a newly Nazified form of traditional Muslim Jew-hatred through Arab translations of *Mein Kampf*—rendered in Arabic as "My Jihad"—and other Nazi anti-Semitic works, including *Der Stürmer* hate cartoons, adapted to portray the Jew as the demonic enemy of Allah.[4]

When World War II finally broke out, al-Banna worked to formalize the Brotherhood's alliance with Hitler and Mussolini. He sent them letters and emissaries, and urged them to assist him in his struggle against the British and the Westernized regime of Egypt's King Farouk. The intelligence service of the Muslim Brotherhood vigorously collected information on the heads of the regime in Cairo and on the movements of the British army, offering this and more to the Germans in return for closer relations.

ENTER THE PALESTINIANS

The best-known and most active Nazi sympathizer in the Muslim Brotherhood was not Hassan al-Banna himself, but Haj Amin al-Husseini, Grand Mufti of Jerusalem and onetime president of the Supreme Muslim Council of Palestine. Haj Amin was a bridge figure responsible for transplanting the Nazi genocide from wartime Europe into the postwar Middle East and creating a fascist heritage for the Palestinian national movement.

Something of a child prodigy, Amin al-Husseini was born into the rich and influential Husseini clan in 1895. He became a powerful anti-Jewish agitator and rabble rouser while still in his early twenties, and then suddenly, by fiat, was chosen as the Grand Mufti of Jerusalem at the age of twenty-seven. It was an unlikely occurrence: A mufti was typically an elected religious leader with great spiritual status and influence. When Jerusalem's preceding mufti, Kamel al-Husseini, died in March of 1921, he should have been replaced by the accepted Ottoman process whereby a careful choice was made from among three worthy and experienced candidates nominated by the Supreme Muslim Council. But figures in the British Mandatory government who were anxious to blunt the growing Zionism in the region elevated the Jew-hating al-Husseini to this position without seeking consensus, although he had been sentenced to ten years in prison for his role in inciting the anti-Jewish riots of 1919 and 1920, in which scores of Jews in Jerusalem and Jaffa were attacked, raped, and killed.

Al-Husseini used his new office as a powerful bully pulpit from which to preach anti-Jewish, anti-Zionist, and (turning on his patrons) anti-British vitriol. He was directly involved in organizing the 1929 riots that destroyed the 3,000-year-old Jewish community of Hebron. And he was quick to see that he had a natural ally in Hitler and in the rising star of Nazi Germany.

In the early 1930s, as many Arabs in British Mandatory Palestine looked toward an alliance with Hitler as leverage against Britain, al-Husseini enthusiastically led the way. In the spring of 1933, when Hitler's rule was still in its infancy, he assured the German consul in Jerusalem that "the Muslims inside and outside Palestine welcome the new regime of Germany and hope for the extension of the fascist, anti-democratic governmental system to other countries."

The youth organization established by the mufti used Nazi emblems, names, and uniforms. Germany reciprocated by setting up scholarships for Arab students, hiring Arab apprentices at German firms, and inviting Arab political leaders to the Nuremberg party rallies and Arab military leaders to Wehrmacht maneuvers. Most significantly, the German Propaganda Ministry developed strong links with the mufti and with Arabic newspapers, creating a propaganda legacy that would outlast al-Husseini, Hitler, and all the other figures of World War II.[5]

In September 1937, Adolf Eichmann and another SS officer carried out an exploratory mission in the Middle East lasting several weeks, and including a friendly visit with the mufti. It was after this visit, in fact, that Haj Amin went on the Nazi payroll as an agent and propagandist.

During the "Great Arab Revolt" of 1936–1939, the war against the Jews of Palestine and against the British enforcement of the Mandate, which Haj Amin helped organize and which Germany funded, the swastika was used as a mark of identity on Arabic leaflets and graffiti. Arab children welcomed each other with the Hitler salute, and a sea of German flags and pictures of Hitler were displayed at celebrations. The identification was so strong that those obliged to travel through areas involved in the Palestinian revolt soon learned that it was prudent to attach a swastika to their vehicle to gain immunity from Arab snipers. The mufti declared certain zones in Palestine to be "liberated" from the Jews and the British, and to be under the authority of Shari'a, the Islamic religious law. Christian as well as Muslim women were forced to veil themselves. Opponents were liquidated.

By 1938, al-Husseini fielded some ten thousand fighters, an active propaganda unit, and modern weapons, thanks in large part to Nazi money and military assistance. But if the mufti was ready for the war that would soon engulf the world, so were the British, who sent massive reinforcements to put down his revolt. Al-Husseini fled to Lebanon, still under French rule, before he could be arrested.

From his safe perch in Beirut, al-Husseini traveled to Berlin in May 1941. From there, he worked tirelessly in behalf of Germany and Nazism. He played a pivotal behind-the-scenes role in instigating a pro-Nazi coup in Iraq in 1941, urging Nazis and pro-Nazi governments in Europe to transport Jews to death camps, and training pro-Nazi Bosnian Muslim brigades. His Muslim Hanjar ("Dagger") division was credited with the murder of approximately 90 percent of Bosnian Jewry. He became a familiar voice on Germany's Arabic-language radio propaganda station, broadcasting from the town of Zeesen near Berlin, to convince Arabs and Muslims in Europe (and especially the Muslim populations of the Balkans and Albania) that they and the Nazis were brothers, and that these two kindred peoples needed to unite against their common enemy: the Jews.[6]

After meeting with Hitler on November 21, 1941, al-Husseini praised the Nazis because they "know how to get rid of the Jews, and that brings us close to the Germans and sets us in their camp." On March 1, 1944, the mufti called out in a broadcast from Zeesen: "Arabs! Rise as one and fight for your sacred rights. Kill the Jews wherever you find them. Kill them with your teeth if need be. This pleases God, history, and religion. This saves your honor." His goal was, with the help of the Nazis, "to solve the question of the Jewish elements in Palestine and in other Arab countries as required by national interests, and in the same way as the Jewish question in the Axis lands is being solved." His own memoirs, and the testimony of German defendants at the

Nuremberg trials, later showed that he planned a death camp modeled on Auschwitz to be constructed near Nablus for the genocide of British Mandatory Palestine's Jews.[7]

The foremost Muslim spiritual leader of his time did all he could to ensure that the Germans focused their energies and resources on the "Final Solution." And he helped in his own way by lobbying to prevent Jews from leaving Hungary, Romania, and Bulgaria, even though the governments of these countries were initially willing to let them go. Eichmann himself recounted: "We have promised him [the mufti] that no European Jew would enter Palestine any more."[8]

But Germany's defeat in North Africa meant that the *Einsatzgruppen*, which had murdered more than one million of the six million Jewish victims of the Holocaust, never took its ghastly show to Palestine. Al-Husseini's boundless ambitions against both Palestinian and world Jewry were halted—he believed only temporarily—by the German surrender on May 8, 1945.

The mufti suddenly found himself a prisoner of war in France, and condemned as a war criminal by the Nuremberg prosecutors. To harm American and especially British interests, the French allowed him to escape. He fled first to Egypt and later to Syria. From Damascus, Haj Amin al-Husseini reestablished himself as the foremost spokesman for the Arabs of Palestine.

A few years later, when the partition of Palestine and the creation of Israel came before the United Nations, al-Husseini joined Hassan al-Banna in urging the Arab world to unite in opposition. The two men saw in the UN resolution an example of the "Jewish world conspiracy," even though the plan provided for an Arab state in Palestine alongside the

David Meir-Levi

Jewish one. Far more important than a state for the Arabs of Palestine was the eradication of Zionism and the annihilation of Palestine's Jews.

No Arab head of state had the courage to contradict al-Husseini in his rejectionism, and the Arab world's enthusiastic reception of his message of hate and genocide ended any possibility of the peaceful implementation of the UN resolution and the creation of an Arab and a Jewish state side by side in the Palestine Mandate. Seventy-four percent of the Mandate had already been allocated to Jordan, whose population was more than two-thirds Palestinian Arab.

As the armies of Egypt, Jordan, Iraq, Syria, Lebanon, Saudi Arabia, and Morocco invaded Israel in 1948, the secretary-general of the Arab League, Abd al-Rahman Azzam (A.K.A. Azzam Pasha), who had previously stated privately that he considered the partition of Palestine to be the only rational solution, now changed his position so that he stood shoulder to shoulder with the mufti. "This war," he declared on the day of the Arab attack, "will be a war of destruction." It was; but it was the armies assembled by the Arabs, many of whom had fought alongside Rommel in behalf of the Third Reich, that were destroyed.

Haj Amin al-Husseini's Nazi ambitions, even though they were now seen against the backdrop of the Holocaust that he had helped in his small way to engineer, continued to be a source of pride for his Arab supporters after his death in 1974. And he found admirers elsewhere too in the decades ahead. Professor Edward Said praised al-Husseini, former partner with the Nazis in their crimes against humanity, as "the voice of the Palestinian people." Yassir Arafat, a distant cousin of al-Husseini, referred to him as "our hero."[9]

12

Transplanting the Pathology: Sayyid Qutb

Nazism might have been eradicated in Europe after World War II, but it was still alive and well in the Arab world. The new amalgam of Nazi and Muslim Jew-hatred created by the preaching of al-Banna and al-Husseini continued to grow in influence. As it did, extremist intellectuals and imams created a fascist form of Islam to justify their ideology. The chief architect of the new Islamic fascism was the supreme ideologue of the Muslim Brotherhood, Sayyid Qutb.

Born in southern Egypt in 1906 and educated in traditional Islam and Qur'anic studies, Qutb moved to Cairo as a boy and there received a secular and Westernized education between 1929 and 1933. After working for a time as a teacher, he became a functionary in Egypt's Ministry of Education in 1939. From 1948 to 1950 he was in the United States on a scholarship to study the educational system, receiving a master's degree from the Colorado State College of Education (now the University of Northern Colorado) and developing both a fascination and a hatred for what he regarded as Western decadence as manifested in its egalitarianism, economic laissez faire, female social equality, and especially the "sinful mingling" of the sexes in the workplace, the marketplace, and even in churches.

In later works, Qutb would describe American society as "a shocking mixture of materialism, lust, and egoistical individualism . . . [and] sale of women and savage racism." He concluded that the United States was engaged in a "new Crusade," waging a subtle, almost subliminal sociocultural war against Islam by undermining Muslim society throughout the world with an eye toward bringing an end to the Islamic religion itself. All of this led Qutb to preach a race hatred as virulent as anything in Nazism:

> The white man in Europe or America is our number one enemy. The white man crushes us underfoot while we teach our children about his civilization, his universal principles and noble objectives. . . . We are endowing our children with amazement and respect for the master who tramples our honor and enslaves us. Let us instead plant the seeds of hatred, disgust, and revenge in the souls of these children. Let us teach these children from the time their nails are soft that the white man is the enemy of humanity, and that they should destroy him at the first opportunity.

But however depraved America was, Qutb would declare in his seminal essay, "Our Struggle Against the Jews," that it was the Jew who was the root of all the world's evil. Picking up on the Nazi ideology he ingested as a member of the Brotherhood, Qutb wrote that Jews were responsible for the world's moral decay and for the West's animalistic sexual depravity. It was the Jews who had created the anti-Islamic doctrines of atheistic materialism, godless socialism, and democratic individualism. The Jews, therefore, were the perpetual enemies of Islam. This essay, arguably the single most important manifesto of Islamic fascist anti-Semitism in the modern world, was distributed in millions of copies throughout the Islamic world with the help of the Wahhabi Islamic sect in Saudi Arabia.

When he returned to Egypt in 1950, Qutb joined the

Muslim Brotherhood and became editor-in-chief of its weekly, *Al-Ikhwan al-Muslimin,* and later head of its propaganda section. His popularity soon brought him to the highest levels of leadership in the Brotherhood, while his writings gave philosophical stature to the organization's Nazi goals. As he saw it, the confrontation between the secular West and the Muslim world was over Islam and nothing but Islam. The confrontation arose from the effort by Christians (referred to as "Crusaders" in his works) and world Zionism to annihilate Islam—a case of projection if ever there was one. The motivation for this ideological war, Qutb asserted, was that the Crusaders and the Zionists knew that their religions were inferior to Islam. They needed, therefore, to annihilate Islam so as to keep it from defeating their own flawed and failed doctrines and attaining victory over the hearts and minds of the entire world. That victory, however, was inevitable. But first, Qutb and the Muslim Brotherhood must "open people's eyes" to the danger that modernity and Western culture and Judaism and Zionism posed.

Among the most dangerous perpetrators of that threat were the treasonous Muslims who were corrupted by Western influences to the point where they could no longer be called Muslims. And the Egyptian dictator Gamal Abdel Nasser was the apotheosis of such corruption. Hence he and his regime must be eliminated.

After the Brotherhood's attempt on Nasser's life in 1953, Qutb was sentenced to fifteen years in prison. Political pressure from Iraq motivated Nasser to free Qutb in 1964; but only eight months later he was arrested again for plotting to overthrow the state. This time, his trial culminated in a death sentence; in August 1966 he was executed by hanging.

Qutb left behind twenty-four books, including novels, contemplations, works of literary criticism, and his two most important and influential tomes: *In the Shade of the Koran* and *Milestones in the Road*. One consistent message of all his work involved adapting fascism to Islamic society and governance: the violent and uncompromising over-throw of insufficiently "pure" secular regimes by terrorism and armed revolution; and the imposition of his interpreta-tion of Islam by force on all Arab peoples, and ultimately the entire world, through jihad.

His books, his role in the Muslim Brotherhood, and his martyrdom as a Muslim hero have made Sayyid Qutb the ideologue par excellence for every Islamofascist movement in the world today. His greatest impact has been through his influence on al- Qaeda, via the work of his brother, Muham-mad, who moved to Saudi Arabia following his release from prison in Egypt. There Muhammad Qutb became a profes-sor of Islamic studies and edited, published, and promoted his brother Sayyid's works. One of Muhammad Qutb's stu-dents was Ayman al-Zawahiri, the number two man in al-Qaeda and one of the most wanted terrorists in the world today.[10]

HITLER "DID NOT FINISH THE JOB"

In her report on the trial of Adolf Eichmann in 1961, Han-nah Arendt commented on the incredible degree to which anti-Jewish vitriol and praise for Hitler, mixed with regret that "he did not finish the job," dominated the news reports in the Arab press. "The newspapers in Damascus and Beirut, in Cairo and Jordan did not conceal either their sympathy

for Eichmann nor their regret that he 'did not finish the job.'
A radio broadcast from Cairo on the opening day of the trial
even included a little sideswipe at the Germans, reproach-
ing them for the fact that 'in the last war, no German plane
had ever flown over and bombed a Jewish settlement.'"

Four decades later, the same qualified homage to Hitler
and the earnest desire to see all Jews annihilated was
expressed in the second-largest, state-controlled Egyptian
daily *Al-Akhbar* (April 18, 2001): "Our thanks go to the late
Hitler, who wrought, in advance, the vengeance of the Palestinians upon the most despicable villains on the face of the
earth. However, we rebuke Hitler for the fact that the vengeance was insufficient."

The long legacy of Arab and Palestinian Nazism, and the
Hitlerite themes of Lebensraum, ethnic cleansing and genocide initiated by the Muslim Brotherhood at its founding,
continue to echo in the Middle East today. Hassan Nasrallah,
leader of Hezbollah, said of the Jews after the Lebanon war
of 2006: "If they gather in Israel, it will save us the trouble
of going after them worldwide." Mahmoud Zahar, the Hamas
foreign minister, says: "I dream of hanging a huge map of
the world on the wall at my Gaza home which does not
show Israel on it." And most chillingly, Ali Akbar Hashemi
Rafsanjani, former president of Iran, looks ahead to the next
holocaust and final solution: "The use of a nuclear bomb in
Israel will leave nothing on the ground, whereas it will only
damage the world of Islam."[11]

ALTHOUGH MANY NAZIS found new and ideologically
welcoming homes in Egypt and Syria after World War II,
the Grand Mufti's Palestinian national movement itself,
bereft of its Nazi patron, was an orphan. No sovereign state
of any consequence supported it. On the contrary, most of
the surrounding Arab states, all of them buoyed by post-
colonial nationalism and looking for political stability, per-
ceived the Palestinian cause, especially as embodied in the
Muslim Brotherhood, as a threat. Egypt aggressively sup-
pressed the Brotherhood. Saudi and Jordanian royalty
watched the growth of radical Islam with suspicion. Syria
and Lebanon, trying to move toward more open societies in
the pre-Ba'athist era, feared the Brotherhood's opposition
to Western-style civil rights and liberties and its fierce condemnation of Westernized Arab societies.

More to the point, each of these states coveted some or
all of what was formerly British Mandatory Palestine and
were no more enthusiastic about the creation of a new Arab
state there than they were about the creation of Israel. As a
result of these complex national ambitions and antago-
nisms, no state for the Arabs of British Mandatory Palestine
was created. Even though Israel offered the return of territories gained in the 1948 war at the Rhodes armistice conference of February 1949, the Arab leaders (among whom

there were no representatives from the Arabs of the former Palestine) rejected Israel's peace offers, declared jihad, and condemned the Arab refugees to eternal refugee status, while also illegally occupying the remaining areas that the United Nations had envisioned as a Palestinian state—as Arafat himself tells us in his authorized biography (Alan Hart, *Arafat: Terrorist or Peace Maker?*). Egypt herded Palestinian Arabs into refugee camps in its new fiefdom in the Gaza Strip, assassinated their leaders, and shot anyone who tried to leave. Jordan illegally annexed the West Bank and maintained martial law over it for the next nineteen years.

Egypt was particularly conscious of the threat the Muslim Brotherhood posed to the Westernized and increasingly secularized society it was trying to build, and both King Farouk and later Gamal Abdel Nasser took brutal and effective steps to repress the movement. They also made sure that the 350,000 Palestinians whom the Egyptian army had herded into refugee camps in Gaza would develop no nationalist sentiments or activism. Egyptian propaganda worked hard to redirect the Palestinians' justifiable anti-Egypt sentiments toward an incendiary hatred of Israel. Its secret police engineered the creation and deployment of the *fedayeen* (terrorist infiltrators) movement, which between 1949 and 1956 carried out over nine thousand terror attacks against Israel, killing more than six hundred Israelis and wounding thousands. These *fedayeen* were mostly Arab refugees, trained and armed by Egypt.

As the conflict with Israel hardened throughout the 1950s, Nasser came to see that Palestinian nationalism, if carefully manipulated, could be an asset instead of just a threat and an annoyance. Although the *fedayeen* terrorism

19

David Meir-Levi

prompted Israel to invade the Sinai in 1956, the Egyptian leader saw the value in being able to deploy a force that did his bidding but was not part of Egypt's formal military; which could make tactical strikes and then disappear into the amorphous demography of the West Bank or the Gaza Strip, giving Egypt plausible deniability for the mayhem it had created. But Nasser's ability to support such a useful terrorist group was limited by the failed economy over which he presided; and so, in 1964, he was delighted to cooperate with the Soviet Union in the creation of the Palestine Liberation Organization (PLO).

Brainchild of the KGB

As Ion Mihai Pacepa, onetime director of the Romanian espionage service (DIE), later explained, the PLO was conceived at a time when the KGB was creating "liberation front" organizations throughout the Third World. Others included the National Liberation Army of Bolivia, created in 1964 with help from Ernesto "Che" Guevara, and the National Liberation Army of Colombia, created in 1965 with help from Fidel Castro. But the PLO was the KGB's most enduring achievement.[1]

In 1964, the first PLO Council, consisting of 422 Palestinian representatives handpicked by the KGB, approved the Soviet blueprint for a Palestinian National Charter—a document drafted in Moscow—and made Ahmad Shukairy, the KGB's agent of influence, the first PLO chairman. The Romanian intelligence service was given responsibility for providing the PLO with logistical support. Except for the arms, which were supplied by the KGB and the East German

20

Stasi, everything, according to Ion Pacepa, "came from Bucharest. Even the PLO uniforms and the PLO stationery were manufactured in Romania free of charge, as a 'comradely help.' During those years, two Romanian cargo planes filled with goodies for the PLO landed in Beirut every week."

The PLO came on the scene at a critical moment in Middle East history. At the Khartoum conference held shortly after the Six-Day War, the defeated and humiliated Arab states confronted the "new reality" of an Israel that seemed unbeatable in conventional warfare. The participants of the conference decided, among other things, to continue the war against Israel as what today would be called a "low-intensity conflict." The PLO's Fatah forces were perfect to carry out this mission.

The Soviets not only armed and trained Palestinian terrorists but also used them to arm and train other professional terrorists by the thousands. The International Department of the Central Committee of the Communist Party (CPSU), the Soviet Security Police (KGB), and Soviet Military Intelligence (GRU) all played major roles in this effort. From the late 1960s onwards, moreover, the PLO maintained contact with other terror groups—some of them neo-Nazi and extreme right-wing groups—offering them support and supplies, training and funding.[2]

The Soviets also built Moscow's Patrice Lumumba People's Friendship University to serve as a base of indoctrination and training of potential "freedom fighters" from the Third World. More specialized training in terrorism was provided at locations in Baku, Odessa, Simferopol, and Tashkent. Mahmoud Abbas, later to succeed Yassir Arafat as head of the PLO, was a graduate of Patrice Lumumba U, where he received his Ph.D. in 1982 after completing a thesis partly based on Holocaust denial.

Cuba was also used as a base for terrorist training and Marxist indoctrination, part of a symbiotic relationship between its revolutionary cadre and the PLO. The Cuban intelligence service (DGI) was under the direct command of the KGB after 1968. Palestinian terrorists were identified in Havana as early as 1966; and in the 1970s DGI representatives were dispatched to PLO camps in Lebanon to assist terrorists being nurtured by the Popular Front for the Liberation of Palestine (PFLP). In late April 1979, an agreement was reached for the PFLP to have several hundred of its terrorists trained in Cuba, following a meeting between its chief George Habash and Cuban officials.[3]

The PLO and the Arab States[4]

In the chaotic aftermath of the Six-Day War, Yassir Arafat had seen an opportunity for himself and his still embryonic Fatah terror organization in the rubble of the Arab nations' war machines and the humiliation of the Arab world. He forged an alliance with President Nasser, whom he won over to his belief that after traditional warfare had failed them yet again, the future of the conflict for the Arabs was in the realm of terrorism, not the confrontation of massed armies.

From September to December 1967, Nasser supported Arafat in his attempt to infiltrate the West Bank and to develop a grassroots foundation for a major terror war against Israel. These efforts were unsuccessful because local West Bank Palestinians cooperated with Israel and aided in the pursuit of Arafat and his Fatah operatives.

Despite such setbacks, Arafat later described this era in his authorized biography as the time of his most successful statecraft. When word reached him of Israel's post-Six-Day-War peace overtures to the recently defeated Arab countries, he and his adjutants understood at once that if there were ever peace between Israel and Jordan, for instance, there would be no hope for a Palestinian state. So he set off on a grueling exercise in shuttle diplomacy throughout the major Arab countries, preaching the need to reject unconditionally any peace agreement with the Jewish state. Arafat later claimed credit for the results of the Khartoum conference (August–September 1967), in which all the Arab dictators unanimously voted to reject Israel's offer to return much of the land it had occupied as a result of the war in exchange for peace. Had he not intervened, Israel might conceivably have made peace with Jordan, and the West Bank would have reverted to Jordanian sovereignty, leaving his dream of leading a state there stillborn.

But while Arafat's proposals to engage in a continuing terror war might be enthusiastically received by Arab leaders, there was no support to speak of among the Arabs of the West Bank, who readily gave him up to Israeli authorities. Arafat was forced to flee with the Israel Defense Forces hot on his trail, and finally established a base for his force in the city of Salt, in southwestern Jordan. From there he executed terrorist raids across the Jordan River and began to set up clandestine contacts with officers in the Jordan Legion, almost half of whom were Palestinians.

The Israeli army, under the direction of Moshe Dayan, launched a limited invasion of Jordan in March 1968 to stop Arafat's raids. Its objective was the village of Karama, near the Jordan River, where most of Arafat's men were encamped. The raid took a terrible toll of terrorist fighters. When Jordanian artillery forces, under the command of Palestinians, unexpectedly opened fire on the Israeli force, the Israelis retreated, not wishing to escalate the raid into a confrontation with Jordan.

Showing his brilliance as a propagandist, Arafat redefined Israel's strategic retreat into a rout. Organizing his defeated and demoralized force into a cavalcade, he marched into Salt with guns firing victoriously in the air, claiming in effect that it was his force, rather than fear of a diplomatic incident, that had caused the Israelis to move back. Arafat claimed that he had liberated both Palestinian and Jordanian *karameh* ("dignity" in Palestinian Arabic) by smashing the Israeli force and driving it back across the Jordan River in shame and disarray. It was pure fiction, but the Arabs believed it. Soon money and recruits were pouring in, and Arafat was able to reconstitute and equip his haggard Fatah force.

Shrewdly leveraging his "victory," Arafat challenged Ahmad Shukairy as head of the PLO in February 1969. Acting through Nasser, the Soviets backed Arafat and he emerged as the unchallenged leader of the Arab terrorist war against Israel. While remaining distinct organizations, the PLO and Fatah were unified beneath the umbrella of his leadership.

At this point, Soviet involvement became critical. Under Russian tutelage, Arafat signed the "Cairo Agreement" in November 1969, which allowed him, with overt Egyptian and Syrian backing and covert Russian support, to move a large part of his force into southern Lebanon. There they set up centers of operation to prepare for terror attacks against

Israel's northern border, while Arafat and the rest of his force remained in Jordan.

The three years of Arafat's sojourn in Jordan were not without internal problems. Fatah terrorists routinely clashed with Jordanian soldiers (more than nine hundred armed encounters between 1967 and 1970). Arafat's men used Mafia tactics to smuggle cigarettes, drugs, and alcohol, and to extort money from local Jordanians, setting up road-blocks to exact tolls and kidnapping notables for ransom to finance "the revolution." When Jordanian forces tried to keep order, Fatah engaged and in some cases killed them.

Jordan's King Hussein was not eager for a confrontation. Faced with Arafat's threats of civil war, he offered the PLO leader a position in the Jordanian parliament. Arafat refused, saying that his only goal in life was to destroy Israel.[5] When the U.S. assistant secretary of state, Joseph Cisco, came to Jordan in April 1970, Arafat organized massive anti-American riots throughout the country, during which one American military attaché was murdered and another kidnapped. Humiliated before his most important ally, Hussein did nothing.

In July 1970, Egypt and Jordan accepted U.S. secretary of state William Rogers' plan for Israel's withdrawal from the West Bank and Gaza in exchange for peace and recognition. But instead of embracing the plan and taking control of the West Bank and Gaza, Arafat denounced the Rogers proposal, reiterating his determination to reject any peace agreement. He then organized riots throughout Jordan in order to prevent a political solution. The liberated Palestine he sought would stretch from the Jordan River to the sea, with no Israel, and could only be achieved through fire and blood.

All peace agreements that left Israel intact were in his view betrayals of the Palestinian cause.

Nasser was furious and let King Hussein know that he had withdrawn his support for Arafat. Blundering ahead, Arafat announced it was now time to overthrow King Hussein, and he launched an insurrection.

Throughout August 1970, fighting between Arafat's forces and the Jordan Legion escalated. Arafat looked forward to support from Syria when he launched his final coup, but the Syrians had backed off because they had learned that the United States had given Israel a green light to intervene if they became involved.

The final straw came on September 6, 1970, when the Popular Front for the Liberation of Palestine (PFLP), nominally under Arafat's control, skyjacked one Swiss and two American airliners. Two of the planes landed in Jordan, where they were emptied of their passengers and then blown up. The passengers were held as hostages, to be released in exchange for PLO and other terrorists in Israeli jails. At this point, King Hussein declared martial law, and ordered Arafat and his men out of Jordan. Arafat responded by demanding a national unity government with himself at its head. Hussein then ordered his 55,000 soldiers and 300 tanks to attack PLO forces in Amman, Salt, Irbid, and all Palestinian refugee camps.

In eleven days it was over. Seeing his forces tottering on the brink of total defeat and perhaps annihilation, Arafat, having promptly fled to safety in Sudan, agreed to face a tribunal of Arab leaders who would adjudicate an end to the conflict. After six hours of deliberation, the rulers of Egypt, Kuwait, Lebanon, Libya, Saudi Arabia, and Sudan decided in favor of King Hussein. And to make matters worse, Arafat's last patron, the dictator Nasser, died of a heart attack while seeing members of the tribunal off at the Cairo airport.

As Hussein forced the remaining PLO terrorists out of his cities, Arafat had no choice but to leave. By March 1971, he had made his way clandestinely to Lebanon, the only Arab country too weak to throw him out.

Once in Lebanon, he sought to take control of the PLO forces, but he discovered that his chief surviving officers quite correctly blamed him for the Jordan debacle, which had become known as "Black September." Their resentment for the great and senseless loss of life in Jordan led to two attempts on his life.

Arafat not only survived, but was able to use his ample diplomatic skills to turn the tables on his opponents inside Fatah and the PLO. He argued that in the few short years that he had led his liberation army, he had awakened Palestinian nationalism (in fact, he had virtually invented it), recruited and armed a substantial terror army (the PLO forces in Lebanon were unscathed by the Black September catastrophe), initiated war against Israel, rebuffed efforts by Egypt and Syria to control the PLO, made his organization into a state within a state in both Jordan and Lebanon, and raised substantial support from a growing number of rich expatriate Palestinians and supporters throughout the Arab world. By early 1971, despite the animosity that his debacle in Jordan had engendered, he successfully reestablished himself as the unchallenged PLO military and political leader.

Arafat's ability to stay at the top of Fatah and the PLO in Lebanon was the result, at least in part, of the support he received from the USSR. Soviet interest in Arafat was motivated largely by his success in organizing and motivating his terrorist followers. The Soviet Union's Cold War agenda required someone with just those talents to expand and develop the terror arm of Soviet activity in the Third World, and especially in the Muslim world. Within a few years, Russian-trained PLO operatives were manning a dozen terror-training camps in Syria and Lebanon, and deploying terror cells across the globe from Germany to Nicaragua, Turkey to Iran.[6]

By 1973, Arafat was a Soviet puppet (and would remain such until the fall of the USSR). His adjutants, including Mahmoud Abbas, were being trained by the KGB in guerrilla warfare, espionage, and demolition; and his ideologues had gone to North Vietnam to learn the propaganda Tao of Ho Chi Minh.[7]

THE PLO DISCOVERS "WARS OF NATIONAL LIBERATION"

As early as 1964, Arafat had sent Abu Jihad (later the leader of the PLO's military operations) to North Vietnam to study the strategy and tactics of guerrilla warfare as waged by Ho Chi Minh. At this time, Fatah also translated the writings of North Vietnam's General Nguyen Giap, as well as the works of Mao and Che Guevara, into Arabic.

Arafat was particularly struck by Ho Chi Minh's success in mobilizing left-wing sympathizers in Europe and the United States, where activists on American campuses, enthusiastically following the line of North Vietnamese operatives, had succeeded in reframing the Vietnam War from a Communist assault on the south to a struggle for national liberation. Ho's chief strategist, General Giap, made it clear to Arafat and his lieutenants that in order to succeed, they too needed to redefine the terms of their struggle. Giap's counsel was simple but profound: the PLO needed to work in a way that concealed its real goals, permitted strategic deception, and gave the appearance of moderation: "Stop talking about annihilating Israel and instead turn your terror war into a struggle for human rights. Then you will have the American people eating out of your hand."

At the same time that he was getting advice from General Giap, Arafat was also being tutored by Muhammad Yazid, who had been minister of information in two Algerian wartime governments (1958–1962):[8]

> Wipe out the argument that Israel is a small state whose existence is threatened by the Arab states, or the reduction of the Palestinian problem to a question of refugees; instead, present the Palestinian struggle as a struggle for liberation like the others. Wipe out the impression ... that in the struggle between the Palestinians and the Zionists, the Zionist is the underdog. Now it is the Arab who is oppressed and victimized in his existence because he is not only facing the Zionists but also world imperialism.

To make sure that they followed this advice, the KGB put Arafat and his adjutants into the hands of a master of propaganda: Nicolai Ceaușescu, president-for-life of Romania. For the next few years, Ceaușescu hosted Arafat frequently and gave him lessons on how to apply the advice of Giap, Yazid, and others in the Soviet orbit. Arafat's personal "handler,"

Ion Mihai Pacepa, the head of the Romanian military intelligence, had to work hard on his sometimes unruly protégé. Pacepa later recorded a number of sessions during which Arafat railed against Ceaușescu's injunctions that the PLO should present itself as a people's revolutionary army striving to right wrongs and free the oppressed: he wanted only to obliterate Israel. Gradually, though, Ceaușescu's lessons in Machiavellian statecraft sank in. During his early Lebanon years, Arafat developed propaganda tactics that would allow him to create the image of a homeless people oppressed by a colonial power. This makeover would serve him well in the West for decades to come.

Although Arafat was pioneering the use of skyjacking during this time and setting off a wave of copycat airborne terrorism, he discovered that even the flimsiest and most transparent excuses sufficed for the Western media to exonerate him and blame Israel for its retaliatory or preventive attacks, and to accept his insistence that he was a statesman who could not control the terrorists he was in fact orchestrating.

But while Arafat was finally absorbing and applying the lessons he learned from his Romanian and North Vietnamese hosts and handlers, as Pacepa describes it in *Red Horizons*, the Soviets still questioned his dependability. So, with Pacepa's help, they created a highly specialized "insurance policy." Using the good offices of the Romanian ambassador to Egypt, they secretly taped Arafat's almost nightly homosexual interactions with his bodyguards and with the unfortunate preteen orphan boys whom Ceaușescu provided for him as part of "Romanian hospitality." With videotapes of Arafat's voracious pedophilia in their vault, and knowing the traditional attitude toward homosexuality in Islam, the KGB felt that Arafat would continue to be a reliable asset for the Kremlin.[9]

Whether or not Arafat's homosexuality was the key to the Soviets' control over him, it is clear that by the early 1970s the PLO had joined the ranks of other socialist anti-colonial "liberation" movements, both in its culture and in its politics; and had reframed its terror war as a "people's war" similar to those of the other Marxist-Leninist terrorist guerrillas in China, Cuba, and Vietnam. Thanks to input from Ceaușescu, General Giap, and the Algerians, Arafat gradually saw the wisdom of jettisoning his fulminations about "throwing the Jews into the sea," and in its place he developed the images of the "illegal occupation" and "Palestinian national self-determination," both of which lent his terrorism the mantle of a legitimate people's resistance. Of course, there was one ingredient missing in this imaginative reconfiguration of the struggle: There had never been a "Palestinian people," or a "Palestinian nation," or a sovereign state known as "Palestine."[10]

CREATING "PALESTINE"

The term Palestine (*Falastin* in Arabic) was an ancient name for the general geographic region that is more or less today's Israel. The name derives from the Philistines, who originated from the Eastern Mediterranean and invaded the region in the eleventh and twelfth centuries B.C. The Philistines were apparently from Greece, or perhaps Crete, or the Aegean Islands, or Ionia. They seem to be related to the Bronze Age Greeks, and they spoke a language akin to Mycenaean Greek.

Their descendants were still living on the shores of the Mediterranean when Roman invaders arrived a thousand years later. The Romans corrupted the name to "Palestina," and the area under the sovereignty of their littoral city-states became known as "Philistia." Six hundred years later, the Arab invaders called the region "Falastin."

Throughout all subsequent history, the name designated only a vague geographical entity. There was never a nation of "Palestine," never a people known as the "Palestinians," nor any notion of "historic Palestine." The region never enjoyed any sovereign autonomy, but instead remained under successive foreign sovereign domains, from the Umayyads and Abbasids to the Fatimids, Ottomans and British.

During the British Mandate period (1922–1948), the Arabs of the area had their own designation for the region: *balad esh-Sham* (the country, or province, of Damascus). In early 1947, in fact, when the UN was exploring the possibility of the partition of British Mandatory Palestine into two states, one for the Jews and one for the Arabs, various Arab political and academic spokespersons vociferously protested against such a division because, they argued, the region was really a part of southern Syria. Because no such people as "Palestinians" had ever existed, it would be an injustice to Syria to create a state *ex nihilo* at the expense of Syrian sovereign territory.[11]

During the nineteen years from Israel's victory in 1948 to Israel's victory in the Six-Day War, all that remained of the territory initially set aside for the Arabs of British Mandatory Palestine under the conditions of the UN partition was the West Bank, under illegal Jordanian sovereignty, and the Gaza Strip, under illegal Egyptian rule. Never during these

32

nineteen years did any Arab leader anywhere in the world argue for the right of national self-determination for the Arabs of these territories. Even Yassir Arafat, from his earliest terrorist days until 1967, used the term "Palestinians" only to refer to the Arabs who lived under, or had fled from, Israeli sovereignty; and the term "Palestine" only to refer to Israel in its pre-1967 borders.

In the PLO's original founding Charter (or Covenant), Article 24 states: "this Organization does not exercise any regional sovereignty over the West Bank in the Hashemite Kingdom of Jordan, in the Gaza Strip or the Himmah area." For Arafat, "Palestine" was not the West Bank or the Gaza Strip, which after 1948 belonged to other Arab states. The only "homeland" for the PLO in 1964 was the State of Israel. However, in response to the Six-Day War and Arafat's mentoring by the Soviets and their allies, the PLO revised its Charter on July 17, 1968, to remove the language of Article 24, thereby newly asserting a "Palestinian" claim of sovereignty to the West Bank and the Gaza Strip.[12]

Part of the reframing of the conflict, along with adopting the identity of an "oppressed people" and "victim of colonialism," then, was the creation, *ex nihilo*, of "historic Palestine" and the ancient "Palestinian people" who had lived in their "homeland" from "time immemorial," who could trace their "heritage" back to the Canaanites, who were forced from their homeland by the Zionists, and who had the inalienable right granted by international law and universal justice to use terror to reclaim their national identity and political self-determination.

That this was a political confection was, perhaps inadvertently, revealed to the West by Zahir Muhse'in, a member of

David Meir-Levi

the PLO Executive Committee, in a 1977 interview with
the Amsterdam-based newspaper *Trouw*.[13]

> *The Palestinian people does not exist. The creation of
> a Palestinian state is only a means for continuing our
> struggle against the state of Israel* for our Arab unity.
> In reality today there is no difference between Jorda-
> nians, Palestinians, Syrians and Lebanese. Only *for
> political and tactical reasons* do we speak today about
> the existence of a Palestinian people, since Arab
> national interests demand that we posit the existence
> of a distinct "Palestinian people" to oppose Zionism.
> [Emphasis added.]

Arafat himself asserted the same principle on many occasions. In his authorized biography he says, "The Palestinian
people have no national identity. I, Yasir Arafat, man of des-
tiny, will give them that identity through conflict with
Israel."[14]

But even these admissions—that the concept of a "Palestinian people" and a "Palestinian homeland" were invented
for political purposes to justify and legitimize terrorism and
genocide—could not stem the enthusiasm of Western leaders. Within the space of a few years, the Middle East conflict
with Israel was radically reframed. No longer was little
Israel the vulnerable David standing against the massive
Goliath of the Arab world. As the PLO's Communist-trained
leaders saw the inroads that Vietnam, Cuba, and other "liberation struggles" had made in the West, Arafat promoted
the same script for the Palestinians. Now it was Israel who
was the bullying Goliath, a colonial power in the Middle

East oppressing the impoverished, unarmed, helpless, hapless, and hopeless Palestinians.

Despite the changing imagery, however, one thing remained constant. From his earliest days, Arafat was clear that the PLO's aim was "not to impose our will on [Israel], but to destroy it in order to take its place . . . not to subjugate the enemy but to destroy him."[15]

The Palestinian nationalism that he and his Communist advisers created would be the only national movement for political self-determination in the entire world, and across all of world history, to have the destruction of a sovereign state and the genocide of a people as its only *raison d'être.*

3 | Islamofascism

THE PLO, FATAH, the PFLP, and the other terrorist groups that carried the Palestinian banner in the 1960s and 1970s gained recruits and power as a result of their redefinition by the Soviets; but the Russian defeat in Afghanistan, after a long and bloody war against mujahideen ("jihad wagers"), created a chasm between Arafat's Soviet backers and the foot soldiers of his terror movement. So Arafat, ever adroit at opportunistically changing tactics when tactics needed changing, looked back to his childhood roots in Egypt after World War II and saw the Muslim Brotherhood and its franchised spin-off in the Gaza Strip, Hamas. With the Soviet Union on the ash heap of history, he now lunged toward radical Islam as a guarantor of the movement for the destruction of Israel.

Neither party in this new alliance was under any illusions. To Sheikh Akhmed Yassin and other Hamas leaders in Gaza, Arafat was of the West—secular, cosmopolitan, Russian trained—in short, that kind of Muslim leader whom the Muslim Brotherhood, whose Palestinian branch Yassin had founded in Hamas, sought to depose and replace with pure fundamentalist Islamists.

To Arafat, Yassin was a radical Islamic ideologue for whom not just Palestinian nationalism but the very concept of nationalism itself was an alien ideology to be obliterated when the time came for the final great jihad. But both shared a hatred of Jews and of Israel, an attraction to terrorism, and the goal of a *Judenrein* Palestine that stretched "from the river to the sea." Destroying the enemy came first; later on they would sort out their respective claims on the governance of the area.

The pragmatic Arafat began to foster the transformation of the Palestinian cause into an Islamic jihad in early 1994 when he returned to Gaza from his twelve-year exile in Tunis, pursuant to the Oslo Accords. He and Yassin put aside their differences and clandestinely joined forces to wage against Israel what would later become known as the Oslo War. The tens of thousands of letters, many bearing Arafat's personal signature, taken from the PLO's Muqat'a (Arafat's fortified compound and main base of operations) in Ramallah during Israel's "Operation Defensive Shield" in the spring of 2002 produced a portrait of Arafat and Yassin colluding in a bad-cop/good-cop type of terror strategy. Hamas would launch an endless stream of terror attacks, including suicide bombings, and Arafat would secretly provide the money and logistical support while claiming to the West that he was doing the best he could to put a lid on terrorism. The deal was simple: Hamas was free to wage its terror war, as long as its operations did not compromise Arafat's political posturing to the international media as an authentic national leader seeking peace and trying to establish rule of law over his unruly religious fanatics who were justly resentful of Israel's violence.

In seeking his marriage of convenience with Hamas, however, Arafat was at risk of undermining his own movement, now defined by secularism and Third Worldism in an era of jihad. Hamas provided the Palestinian people with a far more powerful rationale than the nihilism of Nazism or Marxism's ideology of national liberation ever had. The organization's fanatical religious-ideological framework, deeply rooted in the history of Islam, created a powerful motivation that had been missing in Arafat's tactic-driven ad hoc terrorism: a vision of a reconstituted Caliphate and a unified transnational Umma waging eternal jihad against global unbelief.

Under Soviet tutelage, Arafat had changed the basic equation of the Arab-Israeli conflict by transforming Israel into an imperialist tyrant denying human rights and simple justice to its Palestinian subjects. But in the ideology of Hamas, Israel was more than an oppressor. It was now the embodiment of evil and house of the infidel, condemned to death and destruction by Allah.

To a largely inchoate Palestinian hatred of Israel, Jews, the West, and all things non-Muslim, Hamas brought—or perhaps more accurately, brought back—the Islamic religious imperative for the destruction of all Jews, worldwide. Thus the campaign against Israel was no longer a mundane human war, one of many in which an occupied people strive for their freedom of national self-determination or human rights (as the Soviets had taught Arafat to present these issues to the West). Now the terror war against Israel was part of the cosmic struggle of the believers against global unbelief, part of the ultimate battle of Islam against the infidels, a vital step in the Islamic apocalypse preceding the redemption of the world and the resurrection of the dead. Genocide against Jews was written into the heart of the Hamas Covenant.

Acknowledging as its inspiration Hassan al-Banna,

founder of the Muslim Brotherhood and ally of Adolf Hitler, Hamas also had strands of communism in its DNA, as the language it used in its "Open Letter to America," justifying the attacks of 9/11, suggests:

> You will face the mirror of your history for a long time to come. Thus you will be able to see exactly how much you have oppressed, how corrupt you are, how you have sinned—how many entities you have destroyed, how many kingdoms you have demolished. . . . Do you remember how the blacks lived under your wing? . . . Your white son bound their necks with the fetters of slavery, after hunting them in the jungles and on the coasts of Africa. . . . Have you asked yourself about your actions against your "original" inhabitants, the Indians, the Apaches? Your white feet crushed them and then used their name, Apache, for a helicopter bearing death, demolition, and destruction for anyone with rights who dared to whisper in his own ear that he has those rights. . . .[1]

In Hegelian terms, Hamas had become the synthesis in the development of Palestinian nationalism, blending its Nazi and Communist roots with religious fanaticism to create Islamofascism.

HAMAS IN THEORY AND PRACTICE

If the profile of Hamas only gradually became visible to the West, in the Middle East it was well known as a self-defined religious-apocalyptic terrorist group whose foundational documents preach genocide and world domination by the military and religious forces of Islam.[2] In Arabic, *Hamas* means "zeal." In Hebrew, Arabic's sister language, the same word means "violence." Both definitions fit, but the group's name actually comes from the acronym for *Haraqat al-Muqawama al-Islamiyah*, "the Islamic resistance movement."

As described in its Covenant (or Charter), Hamas is the "Palestinian branch of the Muslim Brotherhood," the movement founded in Egypt in 1928 by al-Banna, whose cornerstone assertion was that true Islam had been diluted and betrayed by Muslim politicians truckling to the West, and that the only way back to the true path was to violently replace these traitorous Muslim politicians with true Islamic leaders who would make the Qur'an their nations' constitutions and Shari'a their civil law. In the world according to al-Banna, once the transnational population of Muslims, the Umma, was under the leadership of right-thinking religious Muslims who eschewed Westernization and modernization, the whole concept of nation-states would dissolve and the Umma would be united, from Mauritania to India, from Turkey to Yemen, and from Pakistan to Somalia, under one Islamic religious Caliphate.[3]

Hamas was formally founded in December 1987, and emerged as a major player in the Arab-Israeli conflict in August 1988 with the publication of its Covenant, under the leadership of the wheelchair-bound Sheikh Akhmed Yassin in Gaza. Along with related material, the Covenant forms the ideological basis for the Hamas commitment to the annihilation of all Jews everywhere in the world. It stresses that the struggle is not only against Israel but against "the Jews" generally.[4]

With its victory in the Palestinian elections of 2006, Hamas became the only democratically elected political power in the world whose foundational agenda includes genocide, and whose sole defining paradigm is terrorism. It is irredentist as well as genocidal, having as part of its longer-term plan the reconquest of those nations that were once under Muslim rule (Spain, Greece, Hungary, Romania, Slovakia, India); and an even longer-range plan of bringing Islam to a position from which it will be "in control of guiding the affairs of life."

THE "SPIRITUAL LEADER"[5]

One key to Hamas' true identity was the character of its maximum leader, Sheikh Ahmed Isma'il Yassin, born in 1936 in the village of al-Jora, near the port city of Ashkelon. His family fled to Gaza during the 1948 war. A sporting accident at the age of fourteen left him paralyzed and wheelchair-bound, although he eventually married and fathered twelve children.

As a student in Egypt, Yassin joined the Muslim Brotherhood and was arrested during a sweep of activists after an attempted coup against President Gamal Abdel Nasser in 1965. Imprisoned and later exiled from Egypt, he returned in 1968 to Gaza, where he became one of the most prominent Muslim Brotherhood figures. He was arrested by Israel in 1984 because of his leadership in arms procurement and was sentenced to thirteen years in prison, but was released the following year as part of the prisoner exchange with Akhmed Jibril's PFLP-GC terrorist organization.

Upon his release, Yassin resumed his work of setting up a military infrastructure, including the stockpiling of weapons for war against Israel. In December 1987, Yassin directed the Brotherhood's expansion and redefinition as Hamas. One of his first achievements as the leader of Hamas was to establish Hamas cells in the West Bank and Jerusalem.

In 1989, once Hamas revealed itself to be a terror group rather than the religious revivalist cult that Israel originally thought it was, Yassin was arrested and charged with murder, possession of weapons, incitement, the illegal transfer of $500,000, assisting the escape of two convicts from prison, recruiting members for Hamas, and membership in an illegal organization. In 1991, he was convicted and sentenced to life imprisonment plus fifteen years. But in 1997, he was released in exchange for two Mossad agents held by Jordan's King Hussein after a failed assassination attempt on another Hamas leader, Khaled Mash'al, in Amman.

During Yassin's imprisonment, the second tier of Hamas leadership, including Musa Abu Marzuq, became the acting leaders of the movement. Hamas then devised a strategy to ensure the continued operation of its leadership. Upon his release from prison in 1997, Yassin resumed his position of leadership, but with a highly structured and fully staffed lower tier of leaders ready to step forward and take his place if necessary.

Yassin led Hamas' rejection of the Oslo Accords and directed a series of terror attacks aimed at disrupting the peace process. Although he was disillusioned with and sometimes disparaging of Arafat's claim to have the ability to achieve victory over Israel in his terror war, Yassin co-operated with the PLO chief and coordinated terror attacks with him. Together they planned attacks that were timed to torpedo peace talks and Palestinian pressure on Arafat to democratize. Being able to blame Hamas, Arafat avoided responsibility and pretended to take steps to rein in the insubordinate terror gangs. The ruse worked for years.[6]

Yassin often proclaimed that his happiest day would be the day he died as a martyr for "the holy cause of Palestine and Jihad." That day came on the morning of March 22, 2004, when an IDF helicopter attack killed him and several of his followers.

THE ROLE OF HAMAS IN THE FIRST INTIFADA (1987–1991)

In its earliest manifestation in Gaza prior to the first Intifada, Hamas was known as *Al-Mujama' al-Islami* ("the Islamic Committee"). It operated primarily against local Palestinians, attacking and sometimes killing those who violated Muslim laws of modesty and also taking punitive action against some criminal elements. Its goal was to purge those who did not conform to strict Muslim religious demands, and to prepare the Gaza Arabs for jihad against Israel. With the outbreak of the first Intifada in December 1987, Hamas also organized street riots and demonstrations, and sent children out to throw stones at Israeli troops.

Ironically, Israel initially ignored the rise of Hamas, and did nothing to stop its growth and spread in the Gaza Strip and the West Bank. Israeli tacticians naively thought that a revivalist religious movement would be a useful counterweight to Arafat's essentially secular PLO. But Israel out-lawed Hamas in 1989, once it began its long series of lethal terror attacks.

To gain popular support, Hamas founded and expanded a system of charitable organizations that provided food, medical centers, and other essentials to the Gazan Arabs. The mosque was its key recruiting venue, and to maintain its image as a religious movement, Hamas organized promi-nent religious leaders into the Association of Religious Sages of Palestine (*Rabitat 'Ulama' Filastin*), which issued religious rulings that confirmed the movement's ideology.[7]

An important factor in Hamas' rapidly developing popu-larity was the fact that Arafat and much of the PLO were in exile in Tunis from 1982 to 1994. Hamas filled the power vacuum that Arafat left behind, serving its impoverished constituency in the refugee camps and providing a religion-based alternative to the secular PLO.

The military apparatus for Hamas' terror activities was structurally separate from the social services. The military arm was called *mujahidin* and named *Izz ad-Din al-Qassam* after an Arab terrorist and member of the Muslim Brother-hood who launched attacks against the British and the Jews during the Mandate period and was "martyred" in 1936. (The Qassam rockets manufactured and deployed by Hamas today are also named after him.) Zaccaria Walid Akel, the head of the terrorist section of Hamas in Gaza, first set up the Izz ad-Din al-Qassam Battalions in 1991. In its early stages the terrorist squads kidnapped and executed people suspected of cooperation with Israel.

Hamas' Alliances[8]

Much of Hamas' success has been the result of support it receives from the Arab and broader Muslim world. Syria became an important base for Hamas activities in the 1990s, providing infrastructure, training camps, and safe harbor for its terrorist leaders. Funding from Iran and Saudi Arabia is easily channeled to the Hamas leadership in Damascus. While at least nominally under Syrian government control until Hafez al-Assad's death, Hamas now operates independently with Iranian support.

Current Iranian leadership has long shared the Hamas vision of a worldwide obliteration of Jews. The Iranian president Mahmoud Ahmadinejad's recent comments about wiping out Israel and destroying the "Great Satan" of America were well received by Hamas leadership in Damascus. In 1993, Hamas opened a branch office in Teheran, and in April 2001 was part of an international conference, hosted by Iran, in support of the "blessed Intifada" and the Islamic revolution in Palestine. The Iranian connection also involves the Lebanese terror group Hezbollah, whose main sponsor is Teheran, and which has also developed a close working relationship with Hamas and has been instrumental in training and equipping its terrorists.

Perhaps the most valuable asset of all for Hamas has been the UN, which has assisted the organization by turning a blind eye to its terrorist interactions with UN personnel. The United Nations Relief and Works Association's ambulances have been photographed being used by Hamas for terror activities. But of even greater value to Hamas is its dominance in UNRWA's workforce. All but a few hundred of UNRWA's twenty-two thousand workers are Palestinians and a good chunk of UNRWA's billions of dollars of salaries flow into the hands of Hamas sympathizers and hence into Hamas terrorist activities.

COORDINATING TERRORISM WITH OTHER GROUPS

While Hamas has always seen itself as a competitor and a religious alternative to the PLO (and later the Palestinian Authority), and as recently as the summer of 2007 engaged in armed conflict with Fatah over the spoils of Palestinian governance, it has also always shared with the PLO the ultimate goal of Israel's destruction and the creation of an Islamic Palestinian state "from the river to the sea." President Clinton might have accepted at face value Arafat's disclaimers about Hamas being a rogue element that he was trying to control, and urged Israel continuously to be more accommodating and supporting of his efforts in that respect; but the West was finally given undeniable proof of this partnership of terror when Israel reoccupied the West Bank in April 2002. Entering Arafat's private compound, the IDF confiscated dozens of computers and hard drives and files, and within a few weeks was able to provide the United States with hard-copy proof of the collusion between Hamas and the PA in tens of thousands of documents, many signed by Arafat's own hand, in which details of logistics between the organizations, finance, planning, timing, and denials were all laid out. At that point, President Bush announced publicly that he no longer considered Arafat to be a meaningful partner for peace.

Hamas also shares long-term strategic objectives with al-Qaeda (their war against what Osama bin-Laden terms "Global Unbelief," with the goal of Islam's global supremacy). In addition to "moral support" and personal interactions, there have been some cases of mutual operational assistance. Israeli intelligence has reported a number of active al-Qaeda cells in the Gaza Strip. With Gaza now open to the Sinai Peninsula, the al-Qaeda cells in Gaza can work with the al-Qaeda terrorist camps in southern Sinai to mount serious military threats to Egypt, Israel, and the entire Eastern Mediterranean.

HAMAS' SUICIDE BOMBER ACADEMY

Hamas' greatest contribution to Arafat's terror war was the development of suicide bombings as a major tactical weapon. Hamas founded a suicide bomber academy in Gaza City, deployed the first suicide bombers in the fall of 1994, and boasted a graduating class of 115 bomber-martyrs in 2001. Between September 2000 and March 2004, Hamas carried out 425 attacks against Israel, 52 of which were suicide bombings; in these attacks, 377 Israelis were killed (288 in suicide bombings) and another 1,646 wounded. Hamas often timed these attacks to critical moments in the "peace talks," knowing that Israel would be forced to halt the Oslo process to formulate a response to the new resurgence of terror.[9]

Unwilling to launch a full-scale military assault on Hamas because of the toll that would inevitably be taken on innocent Palestinians, Israel fought to defend itself against the terror onslaught by "decapitations" of the organization's

David Meir-Levi

leaders. Sheikh Akhmed Yassin and Abdul-Azziz Rantisi were high on the list.

But neither Israel's targeted assassinations nor its diplomatic concessions could change Hamas' views of the war it waged. After Israel's unilateral disengagement from the Gaza Strip in August of 2005, Hamas leader Mahmoud Zahar said: "Neither the liberation of the Gaza Strip nor of the West Bank, nor even Jerusalem, will suffice. Hamas will pursue its armed struggle until the liberation of all of our lands."[10]

THE 2006 ELECTIONS AND
THE MECCA ACCORDS

In the 2006 elections for seats in the Palestinian Legislative Council, Hamas scored a much bigger victory than expected, winning more than half the seats. Hamas emphasized in its electioneering the need to clean up Fatah corruption and mismanagement. As a result, many analysts suggested that the popular vote did not mean that the Palestinians supported Hamas' terrorist agenda, but rather simply longed for efficient garbage collection and honest government. However, Hamas leaders Mahmoud Zahar and Khaled Mash'al stressed repeatedly in post-election speeches that Hamas had "known stances" (genocide of worldwide Jewry, destruction of Israel, creation of a fundamentalist Muslim state based on Shari'a law with non-Muslims reduced to dhimmitude, a subservient status), and therefore the popular vote was an endorsement of these policies. Moreover, many Hamas posters and leaflets used graphic depictions of Hamas terrorists, armed and masked, preparing to "liberate Al-Aqsa" and Jerusalem as part of the electioneering. The message to the Palestinian rank and file was perfectly clear.

But the transfer of power did not go smoothly because Fatah did not want to hand over control of security forces or the PA's money. Growing friction between Hamas and Fatah escalated from localized killings and brief firefights into a bona fide civil war at the end of 2006 and beginning of 2007 and on into the summer of that year, during which more Palestinians were killed than had been killed by Israel in its defensive strikes over the previous six years.

Thanks to its "coup" in Gaza, Hamas now had the political legitimacy and leverage it needed in order to reload, rearm, re-recruit, and redeploy for the great final jihad promised in its Covenant. And its leaders are unabashed in their pronouncements, which tell the world, and especially their Palestinian constituency, exactly what Hamas plans to do.

Mahmoud Zahar lays out the character of the Islamist Palestinian state according to the Hamas vision: "This will be a state which will be based on the principles of the Shari'a and will be part of the Arab Islamist Umma." In the Shari'a-led Palestine, mixed dancing will be prohibited. Homosexuals and lesbians, which Zahar defines as "a minority of moral and mental deviants," will have no rights. "It is in our national interest to stop the cooperation with Israel in any field," says Zahar. Hamas will also use all the weapons in the Palestinian territory to create an Islamist Palestinian state in all of that territory, and use terrorism to obliterate the Israeli state. In response to a question concerning the nature of Palestine under Hamas rule from a *Newsweek* reporter on August 30, 2005, Zahar responded, "It should be Hamastan."

Khaled Mash'al currently continues to espouse Hamas'

long-range plan of Islam's world conquest. At the Al-Murabit Mosque in Damascus on February 3, 2006, as part of a Friday sermon aired on Al-Jazeera, he preached:

> We say to this West, which does not act reasonably, and does not learn its lessons: By Allah, you will be defeated.... The nation of Muhammad is gaining victory in Palestine. The nation of Muhammad is gaining victory in Iraq, and it will be victorious in all Arab and Muslim lands.... These fools will be defeated, the wheel of time will turn, and times of victory and glory will be upon our nation, and the West will be full of remorse, when it is too late....[11]

PART TWO

A key step in Hitler's rise to power in the 1930s was his attack on the Versailles Treaty and his campaign to define the fatherland as a victim. This myth became the justification he used to disarm Europe as he broke all of Germany's arms control agreements, swallowed Austria and Czechoslovakia, and ultimately declared all-out war.

The Palestinians too have presented themselves to the West as victims and have created a similar mythology based on this status to justify their war on Israel. Having seen how Palestinian fascism evolved, we must now dissect the myths it has created to justify this long aggression.

4 | Zionists Stole Our Land

On November 29, 1947, the UN voted into existence two new states: one called Israel for the Jews, and one for the Arabs, which never came into existence and never received a name. What happened? Why was Israel born while its partition counterpart was aborted? This is a crucial question because of the Palestinians' success in propounding the notion that there was no state for the Arabs of British Mandatory Palestine in 1948 solely because of the animosity of the Jews, who heartlessly stole their land. But history provides a different answer.

DESERT TO FARMLAND

Jews became a dominant political force in Israel in the time of Joshua and the Judges about 3,200 years ago. Through the periods of the Monarchy, and even after the Assyrian, Babylonian, Persian, Greek, and Roman conquests, the land maintained its character as a Jewish state.

With the Roman victory and destruction of the Second Temple (70 A.D.), the area came under the sway of Hellenist pagans, then Byzantine Christians, Persians, and finally the Arab Muslim invaders of the early seventh century. For the next eight hundred years, a dozen different empires came

David Meir-Levi

and went; but Islam remained the dominant religion, and Arabic the dominant language. Throughout this period, Jews continued to live in Hebron, Jerusalem, and several other communities in Israel, but only as a barely tolerated minority,[1] part of the dhimmi population of non-Muslims under Muslim rule.

Under the Ottoman Empire (1514–1917) present-day Israel was a neglected backwater. Its population and economy stagnated, and vast tracts reverted to uninhabited desert and swamp. A Turkish census of the mid-nineteenth century counted only about 250,000 people in this very underpopulated area.[2] (To get an idea of what "underpopulated" means in this context, consider that the same area today is home to approximately ten million people, with room for more.)

The poverty and sparse settlement that characterized the previous era was ended by three watershed events at the end of the nineteenth century: The Turks' forcible relocation of non-Muslim subjects from the Balkans, Circassia, and Greece to create a peasantry to work the land and provide a tax base; British interest in the "Holy Land" because of its Christian origins and also to gain a political foothold in the Middle East; czarist pogroms of late nineteenth-century Russia, which drove hundreds of Jews to what became Israel, where they founded the first kibbutz in 1882.

With modern medicine available for the first time, Arab infant mortality decreased and adult longevity increased. British and Zionist construction and development created employment at all levels of the economic ladder, attracting Arab laborers (*fellahin*) by the tens of thousands from sur-

54

rounding areas of Egypt and what would later become the Arab states of Jordan, Syria, Iraq, and Lebanon.

From the 1830s onward, the rulers of the region, Ottoman and Egyptian, forced outside populations—Bulgarians, Circassians, and Arabs from surrounding areas—to relocate into the region because it was largely underpopulated and severely underdeveloped. This policy negatively affected the indigenous Arab fellahin. The newcomers created competition for scarce resources (especially water) and offered new sources of supply for agrarian markets. Fellahin, already reduced to subsistence agriculture, had to work harder to produce what they needed to survive.[3]

In the middle of the nineteenth century, the sultan, ruler of the Ottoman Empire, decreed *Tanzimat*, a series of land reform laws. These new laws radically changed land ownership, allowing wealthy land owners, bankers, business owners, and money lenders anywhere in the Turkish empire to buy land formerly owned communally and inalienably by the Arab farmers of the agrarian towns and villages of the region that would later become known as Israel. Wealthy Arabs (*effendis*) from Cairo to Beirut, Jaffa to Damascus, and points in between purchased vast tracts of land that had previously been inalienable. As a result, untold tens of thousands of fellahin who had once been small-tract land-owning farmers were suddenly rendered into landless serfs who had to work on what was once their own land for the benefit of their new overlords. The Palestinian Arab peasantry watched helplessly as their own land was bought out from under them, by their own people.

———

ZIONISM

As the Tanzimat laws were being implemented, Zionists were beginning to buy land in what would later be called Israel and Transjordan. The land they purchased from the sultan was largely unoccupied and unworked. This rendered no one landless. In fact, it had a positive influence on the neighboring fellahin, since the technologically advanced Zionist agrarian endeavors resulted in the reclamation of arid areas with modern irrigation. Fellahin could graze their flocks on the newly created grassland surrounding the Zionists' fields. In the Jezreel and upper Hula valleys, newly drained swampland created arable tracts beyond the holdings of the Zionists, and local Arabs worked those lands, albeit illegally as squatters in the eyes of the Crown and the effendis.

Zionists also purchased privately owned land. Unlike the effendis, who kept the fellahin on the land as serflike peasants, the Zionists primarily worked the land themselves. In some cases, they paid an additional fee to the land owner to compensate the fellahin's relocation. Since there was much unworked land on both the eastern and the western side of the Jordan River, these fees allowed some fellahin who had been rendered serfs by the Tanzimat to purchase land of their own and once again establish themselves as land-owning farmers.

In some cases when Zionists purchased land that was uninhabited, they discovered the land suddenly covered with Bedouin tents or the shanties of squatters. Having no police or other armed force of their own, they turned to the Ottoman courts. Honest neighbors often testified to the attempted extortion, and the Ottoman law enforcement officials drove the squatters off. Other times, in the absence of such witnesses, the Zionists paid off these squatters or bought land for them elsewhere.

The Hope-Simpson report in 1 9 3 0, addressing the question of uprooted Arab peasants under the British Mandate, concluded that only about eight hundred families were actually rendered landless by Zionist land purchases in the fifty years from 1 8 8 0 onward. On balance, the Zionist endeavor in the late nineteenth and early twentieth centuries was beneficial to the indigenous Arab population, reversing the harsh consequences of Tanzimat and allowing some fellahin to regain their status as land-owning farmers.[4]

UNDER THE BRITISH

British involvement in the Holy Land began in the early decades of the nineteenth century. When the French assisted Mehmet Ali and Ibrahim Pasha in Egypt during their revolts against the Turks, England worked with the sultan to counter the rebellion and then limit the extent of French influence in the Middle East. British support for the sultan came at a price: the entry of English political and cultural representatives into the Holy Land to build schools, hospitals, churches, and other cultural centers.[5]

With the opening of the Suez Canal and the discovery of petroleum in Mesopotamia (later to be known as Iraq), British interest in the region skyrocketed. Eventually the British would build oil refineries in Haifa and a railway connecting the Eastern Mediterranean port with Iraq.

European influence in the region grew when Turkey chose the wrong side in World War I, entering the conflict as Germany's ally. After the Armistice, British and French diplomats carved up the Turkish empire into what they thought would be manageable puppet states. Thus Iraq, Syria, Lebanon, and Hashemite Arabia (later to become Saudi Arabia) were born. Shortly after the war, the League of Nations gave Britain the mandate to occupy the land and develop the social and political infrastructure so that its local population of Arabs and Jews would eventually be able to govern itself.

During the war, the British had promised sovereignty to the Arab leaders in the same areas where they were assuring support to the Zionists who were developing settlements in the hope of someday creating a state. The Balfour Declaration (1917), which said that British policy "looks with favour upon the creation of a Jewish homeland" in Palestine, gave a great moral boost to Zionism but caused considerable consternation among some Arab leaders.

Arab riots in 1919, 1921, 1922, and 1929 took the lives of hundreds of Jews. According to one historian, British military leaders in Palestine (contrary to the intentions and without the knowledge of Whitehall) worked with Arab leaders, and especially Haj Amin al-Husseini (see Chapter One), to plan these riots in order to show the government just how unpopular the UK's pro-Zionist policy was among the Arabs.[6]

In 1922, responding to these Arab pressures and to its promises to the Hashemite dynasty, which had aided its cause in World War I, Britain carved out Transjordan—the area east of the Jordan River, 74 percent of the entire Mandate area—and gave it to the Hashemite Emir Abdullah, who declared that the existing Jewish farming settlements east of the Jordan River must be dismantled and relocated in areas to the west.[7]

As they attacked Jews, Arab leaders also pressured the British to limit Jewish immigration, and won the concession of a series of British "white papers" that substantially reduced the number of Jews allowed to enter Palestine each year.

As Hitler came to power, hundreds of thousands of Jews sought to flee Germany. Denied entry into most other European countries and into the United States, many tried to enter Palestine. This influx enraged the Arabs, who then escalated their terrorism to all-out war against the British and the Jews in 1936, under al-Husseini's leadership, in what later became known as the "Great Arab Revolt."

In the midst of the revolt, the British tried to resolve the situation through diplomacy and compromise. Lord Peel carried out a six-month fact-finding mission and reached the conclusion that Jews and Arabs could not live together. His suggestion was a partition of Palestine: about 15 percent to the Jews and 85 percent to the Arabs.

Jewish leadership gladly accepted Lord Peel's partition plan. Arab leadership was infuriated by the suggestion that any of Palestine be given over to Jewish sovereignty. In response, the Arabs not only rejected the partition plan, but escalated the "Revolt." With war on the horizon and the mufti making overtures to Hitler, the British quickly augmented their military strength and killed somewhere between 3,000 and 10,000 Arabs, bringing the revolt to an end in 1939.

The history of these times is tangled and complex, but one fact clearly emerges: Had Arab leadership accepted the Peel Commission compromise, the Palestinian people would have had their own state in 1937 on about 85 percent of what is today Israel.

WORLD WAR II AND THE HOLOCAUST

With the coming of war, the British position in Palestine was complicated by the fact that Haj Amin al-Husseini (as we have seen) organized tens of thousands of Muslim volunteers to fight in Hitler's army. In an attempt to mollify the Arabs, Britain clamped down even harder on Jewish immigration, thus trapping in Europe hundreds of thousands of Jews who otherwise would have found relative safety in Palestine.

After the war, as the magnitude of the Holocaust emerged, there was even greater pressure for immigration of Jewish survivors. But Britain refused to relent. In defiance, the Jews of Palestine continued to support illegal immigration. Arab leaders, seeing the growth of the Jewish population, renewed their overt terrorist warfare against the Jews, culminating in the horrific car bomb that killed and injured over one hundred people and destroyed much of downtown Jewish Jerusalem in February of 1948. Under the direction of David Ben-Gurion, Jews urged the British to fulfill their obligations to protect the Jewish citizenry of Mandatory Palestine. But several rogue Jewish paramilitary groups began a terror offensive against both the British and the Arabs. The most famous of these was the Lehi organization ("Fighters for the Freedom of Israel"), whose leader, Menachem Begin, later became the first prime minister of Israel to make peace with an Arab country when he and Egypt's Anwar Sadat shook hands at Camp David in 1979.

With no practical solution to the tensions between the Jews and the Arabs, and facing the very heavy economic burden of postwar recovery, Britain's new Labor government began looking for a way to extricate itself from the obligations of "empire" and quickly handed over its Mandate to the newly formed United Nations.

Several UN fact-finding missions visited Palestine in 1947. Lengthy and uninhibited interviews with Jewish leaders, rank-and-file, rich, poor, newcomers, and even refugees aboard the immigrant ships that had been held up by the British, all resulted in the impression that the Jews, especially after the Holocaust, needed a state. To avoid infringing on land owned by Arabs and because of land already legally owned by Jews and the Jewish Agency for Palestine, this state would have to be rather oddly configured, with a segment in the south connected to a sausage-like piece in the middle and a third piece in the north—an administrative, managerial, and security nightmare.

The Arabs, however, insisted that the UN had no jurisdiction over Palestine[8] and refused to meet with fact-finding committees, or agreed to meet and then did not show up. In general, their attitude was quite straightforward and honest: it did not matter what the UN decided because once the British were gone the Arabs would wipe out the Jews and Palestine would be an Arab country, from the river to the sea.

By a tiny margin, the UN partition plan was passed on November 29, 1947. It created two states. The Jewish state was primarily on land that Jews had purchased and developed over the past one hundred years. The Arab state included much of the coastal plain from the Sinai border up to Jaffa, all of the West Bank's central hill country, and most of the Western Galilee. Jerusalem was to be an international city, with the rights of all religions guaranteed by the United Nations and multinational oversight.

Zionists and Jews everywhere rejoiced. The Arabs prepared for war.

Had the Arab world accepted the partition, the Arabs of Palestine would have had a state standing alongside Israel since December of 1947. But rejection of a possible Jewish state was far more important to the leaders of the Arab world than the creation of a state for the Arabs of Palestine.

THE 1948 WAR

As early as the fall of 1947, when the end of the British Mandate was clearly in sight, the Arabs began sporadic attacks against the Jews, who responded in kind. With this early "prewar" violence, tens of thousands of Arabs fled Galilee and the coastal plain. Their numbers were so great that a special Arab summit in Beirut in September 1947 urged all Arab nations to open their doors to these refugees.

The Jewish war of survival began in earnest after the UN endorsed the partition plan on November 29, 1947. Arab mobs and paramilitary forces attacked Jewish settlements across the country. The Jewish response in this first stage of the war was mostly defensive, repelling Arab attacks, but with heavy loss of life. Since the British were officially still in charge until May 14, 1948, no Arab state directly intervened at this time. However, they all sent in thousands of paramilitary fighters. The Haganah, the Jews' defense force, was hampered by the British Mandatory force, which confiscated Jewish weapons (and sometimes turned them over to Arabs) and arrested Haganah activists. Two paramilitary Jewish forces, Irgun and Lehi, carried out attacks against British and Arab targets, giving the British justification for reprisals.[9]

The war went into its second phase on May 14, 1948, with the termination of British control and the creation of the State of Israel. Freed from British obstruction, seven Arab armies (Egypt, Syria, Lebanon, Jordan, Iraq, Saudi Arabia, and Morocco) invaded at once. At the same time, the Haganah began a series of counterattacks. Because of the Haganah's success, the Arab forces agreed to a ceasefire on June 11, 1948.

The Jews utilized this ceasefire to strengthen their positions. The Arab states did the opposite. Their distrust of one another impelled them to keep the majority of their forces on their own borders, in case one neighbor decided to use the confusion of war to enhance its territorial claims at the expense of another.

By the time of the second ceasefire, January 2, 1949, the Israelis had recaptured almost all lost territory, and the Haganah had carried the war to Arab territory, driving Arab armies and irregulars out of much of the territory that the UN had designated as Arab Palestine. In doing so, Israeli forces did not "steal" any land, nor did they violate any international laws or norms. Since Israel later offered to return captured territory during the armistice talks of 1949 (see below), it is false to suggest that Israel fought this war to capture Arab land.

When the fighting was over, approximately 725,000 Arabs had fled. Some anecdotal Arab accounts offered a candid explanation as to why: "We feared that they would do to us what we would have done to them had we won."

Considering the massacres of Jews by Arabs in Hebron, Gush Etzion, and the Jerusalem Jewish Quarter, it is understandable that the Arabs would project their own bloody fantasies onto Israel.

At this time, Arab countries all across North Africa, Egypt, Lebanon, Syria, Iraq, Yemen, and others forcibly expelled their Jewish citizens. In many cases, these were Jews whose families had lived in these countries for more than a thousand years. (In the case of Iraq and Egypt, Jewish communities were documented there from the seventh century B.C.—1,400 years before Muhammad.) Estimates vary, but somewhere between 850,000 and 900,000 Jews were forced from their homes in Arab lands. They left behind property and cash valuing around $2,500,000,000. About 80 percent of these Jewish refugees came to Israel and were absorbed into the new Jewish state.[10]

The New State and *al-Nakba*

Arabs call the unexpected Israeli victory in 1948 *al-Nakba* ("the Catastrophe"). But how responsible was Israel for this disaster? Under threat of annihilation as Arab armies invaded from three fronts at once, Israel employed defensive actions to hold the territory assigned to it by the United Nations. Part of that defensive action included driving Arab civilians from their homes in a few Arab villages located at strategically important sites or sitting upon major arteries, especially the road to Jerusalem. These actions, both legal and commonplace in war since time immemorial (Muhammad is praised for doing the same thing to Jewish villages near Mecca before he besieged it), have been reframed by

Arab propaganda into the first and foundational chapter in the narrative of Israel's aggression against the Palestinians.

We will deal with the issue of refugees in more detail below, but for now it is worth noting the obvious—that the real cause of the refugees' flight was the Arab invasion. Had there been no war, there would have been no refugees. Moreover, had there been any Arab state willing to negotiate peace with Israel after the war, it is very likely that many, if not all, refugees could have returned to their homes in that part of Palestine which the UN had designated for the Arab state. But the Arabs refused to negotiate and refused to create this UN-mandated Arab state.

But Arab culpability for *al-Nakba* goes further. Grabbing the land intended by the UN for the Arabs of Palestine, the forces of Jordan occupied the West Bank, unilaterally and illegally annexing it, while King Farouk of Egypt declared Egyptian sovereignty over the Gaza Strip. Both actions were in violation of international law, in addition to defying UN Resolutions 181 and 194. In addition to illegally occupying land that was supposed to be the Palestinian state, Jordan and Egypt and other Arab states maintained the helpless Palestinian refugees in concentration camps for future use as moral leverage against Israel and the West.

The Arabs who stayed in Israel and became citizens of Israel (approximately 170,000 in 1949, now in excess of 1,400,000) prospered. Today, Arab Israelis serve as members of parliament (the Knesset), faculty in universities, highly educated professionals in just about every field of endeavor, and enjoy a standard of living, political and personal freedom, and economic opportunity unparalleled anywhere in the Arab world.

5 | The Political Abuse of the Refugee Issue

The Arab version of the tragic fate of Arab refugees who fled from British Mandatory Palestine before and during the 1948 war, and from Israel immediately after the war, has so thoroughly dominated the thinking of historians, commentators, journalists, and politicians that it is now commonly accepted that the creation of the State of Israel alone caused the flight of almost a million helpless Arab refugees. Israel caused the problem, so this narrative goes, and thus Israel must solve it before there can be a settlement in the Middle East.

This assertion, canonized by the anti-Israel international left and given currency especially by the United Nations, is unequivocally false, a malicious myth successfully foisted upon the world for political gain by the very Arab states and leaders who were instrumental in causing the refugee problem in the first place.

How the Arabs Left Israel

As early as the fall of 1947, months before the UN partition plan, it was clear that there would be war no matter what course of action the UN took. In anticipation of this war, many of the well-to-do Arabs of the Western Galilee, from Haifa to Acco and villages in between, closed down their houses and went to Beirut or Damascus, where, with their wealth and connections, they could wait for the end of hostilities in safety. They thought that once the war was over (no one imagined that Israel could win), they would come back to their homes. Objective observers estimate that about seventy thousand fled.

The flight of the Arab elite caused a sudden vacuum of political and social leadership among the Arabs of the Galilee, and thus, as the hostilities developed in the winter of 1947, many of the Arab peasantry fled as well, following their leaders' example. Lacking the effendis' money and connections, many of the fellahin simply walked with whatever they could carry to Lebanon or Syria. They too were sure, based upon euphoric reports in the Arab press at the time, that when the war was over and the Jews were all dead or driven out, they would come back to their homes, and to the Jews' abandoned property as well.

There are no solid numbers for this exodus, but estimates suggest it was around a hundred thousand people. The high numbers of those leaving caused the Arab states to call a special conference in Beirut to decide how to handle the hundreds of thousands pouring across the borders. They set up special camps, later to be known as refugee camps.

At this point, neither Israel nor the Arab states were encouraging, frightening, or ordering these masses to flee. The war had not yet even begun.

A War of Survival

After November 29, 1947, warfare between Israeli and Arab paramilitary volunteers numbering in the tens of thousands (trained and armed in Syria and Lebanon, with the aid of both ex-Nazi and British officers) began in earnest. The Arab press and political elite made it clear that this was to be a war of annihilation. The Jews would be either dead or gone from the area. This meant that Israel was not fighting a war of independence, but a war of survival.

To defend some areas where Jews were completely surrounded by Arabs—in Jaffa, for instance, and in Jewish villages or kibbutzim in parts of the Galilee and the central hill country, and in some suburbs of Jerusalem and in the Jewish Quarter of the Old City—the Haganah adopted scare-tactics that were intended to strike terror into the Arab population and make it leave for safer ground, thus making possible the defense of those Jews who would otherwise be vulnerable to the Arabs' genocidal intentions. Many Arabs in the Western Galilee, Jaffa, and parts of West Jerusalem fled because of these tactics, which at times included hand grenades thrown on front porches of homes, drive-by machine-gunning of walls or fences of houses, and rumors circulated by Arabic-speaking Jews that the Haganah was far bigger than it really was and that it would soon appear with a massive Jewish army.

But the Haganah did not set out to ethnically cleanse the country or to wipe out the Arabs. Its actions were undertaken because Jews left undefended in Arab enclaves would be slaughtered (as in fact was the case of Jews in the Gush Etzion villages and in the Jewish Quarter of the Old City in Jerusalem, and as had happened in Hebron in 1929). Fighting a war of survival against a bigger and better-armed enemy narrowed Israel's tactical options.

While the Haganah was trying to force Arabs to leave

Jewish areas that would be difficult to defend, there were a number of cases where Jewish leaders publicly pleaded with Arabs not to leave. At the risk of his own life, the senior Jewish official in Haifa, as well as the Haganah's high command, drove through the Arab section of the city with a loudspeaker on April 26, 1948, calling out in Arabic to the residents of his city to remain on their land and in their homes. A communiqué issued by the Haifa headquarters of the British police noted, "Every effort is being made by the Jews to persuade the Arab populace to stay and carry on with their normal lives, to get their shops and businesses open and to be assured that their lives and interests will be safe."

Arab leaders of the paramilitary forces, and the forces of Syria, were blunt in their announcements that they wanted Arabs to leave these areas—so that the Arab armies would have a clear field in which to perpetrate their genocide of the Jews. When the war was over (Arab newspaper articles at the time suggested that it would take four to six weeks before all the Jews were driven out or killed), the Arab residents could return better off than when they had left. ("We will smash the country with our guns and obliterate every place the Jews seek shelter in," stated the Iraqi prime minister, Nuri Said. "The Arabs should conduct their wives and children to safe areas until the fighting has died down.")

We cannot know for sure how many Arabs fled because of this pressure, but it is clear that their leaders' own message was a major factor in the Arab flight. Five years after the 1948 war, the Jordanian newspaper *Al Urdun* wrote, "For the flight and fall of the other villages it is our leaders who are responsible because of their dissemination of rumors exaggerating Jewish crimes and describing them as atrocities in order to inflame the Arabs.... By spreading rumors of Jewish atrocities, killings of women and children etc., they instilled fear and terror in the hearts of the Arabs in Palestine, until they fled leaving their homes and properties to the enemy."

No honest Arab statesman could deny that this was so. Khaled al-Azm, the Syrian prime minister after the 1948 war, said bluntly in his memoirs published in 1973: "We brought disaster upon a million Arab refugees by inviting them and bringing pressure on them to leave. We have accustomed them to begging ... we have participated in lowering their morale and social level.... Then we exploited them in executing crimes of murder, arson and throwing stones upon men, women and children ... all this in the service of political purposes."

Mahmoud Abbas (Abu Mazen), current leader of the Palestinian Authority, wrote in *Falastin al-Thawra*, the official journal of the Palestine Liberation Organization in 1976: "The Arab armies entered Palestine to protect the Palestinians from the Zionist tyranny, but instead they abandoned them, forced them to emigrate and to leave their homeland, imposed upon them a political and ideological blockade and threw them into prisons similar to the ghettos in which the Jews used to live in Eastern Europe."

The "Massacre" at Deir Yassin

Arab myth makers seeking to prove that Jews are wholly responsible for the Arab refugee situation always come back to Deir Yassin, a village near Jerusalem, overlooking the road from Tel Aviv. The "massacre" that the Israelis supposedly perpetrated there is one of the central exhibits in the Arab argument about refugees, although some Arab leaders have acknowledged that this ambiguous event was concocted to shame the Arab armies into fighting against the Jews, and to frighten Arab citizens and encourage them to flee their homes.

The events that took place at Deir Yassin are still hotly disputed, but this much is known: A contingent of Iraqi troops entered the village on March 13, 1948. They intended to cut off the road to Jerusalem that was the city's lifeline from Tel Aviv and the coastal plain. So on April 9, a contingent of the Irgun (an Israeli paramilitary splinter group) entered Deir Yassin to drive out the Iraqis. Their intentions were no secret. Preceding them was a jeep and loudspeaker telling the civilian population to flee the village. Unfortunately, this jeep slid into a ditch, so some of the villagers may not have heard the message; but many did, because more than two-thirds of the villagers were gone before Irgun soldiers got into Deir Yassin. Rather than surround the village and bar escape, the Irgun left several routes open for the civilians to flee, which hundreds of villagers used.

But the Iraqi soldiers had disguised themselves as women (concealing weapons beneath the flowing robes of the chador) and had hidden among women and children in the village. So when the Irgun arrived, they found themselves taking fire from "women." In the fight that followed, many innocent women did indeed die. The Irgun force suffered more than 40 percent casualties before succeeding in killing or capturing the Iraqi fighters.

When the Haganah (later the Israel Defense Forces)

arrived, it found the dead civilians. Next came the Red Cross, which also found the dead, but no evidence of a "massacre." In fact, even the most recent review of the evidence, by Arab scholars at Beir Zeit University in Ramallah, have admitted that there was no massacre, but rather a confusing military conflict in which civilians were killed in the crossfire. The total Arab dead, including the Iraqi soldiers, according to the Beir Zeit scholars, was 1 0 7.

The same Arab sources that confess to having urged the Arabs to flee have also acknowledged that Arab spokespersons at the time hugely exaggerated the Deir Yassin fight, making up stories of gang rape, brutalities committed against pregnant women, unborn children cut from their mothers' wombs, and massive murders with bodies thrown into a nearby quarry. These same Arab sources admit that their purpose in these exaggerations was to get Arabs to flee the area and also shame the Arab nations into entering the conflict with greater alacrity.

The Arab armies did indeed invade, and Arab civilians did believe the stories of Deir Yassin and fled by the tens of thousands.[1] This is documented by a 1993 (revised 2001) PBS program called *The 50 Years War* in which Deir Yassin survivors were interviewed. They recalled begging Dr. Hussein Khalidi, director of Voice of Palestine (the Palestinian radio station in East Jerusalem) to edit out the lies and fabrications of atrocities that never happened. But he refused, telling them: "We must capitalize on this great opportunity!"

Deir Yassin was not an example; if anything, it was the exception. We have this from an unimpeachable source, Yassir Arafat himself, who said that the Deir Yassin lies were spread "like a red flag in front of a bull" by the Egyptians. Then, having terrorized helpless Arabs with these stories, the Egyptians proceeded to herd them into detention camps in Gaza (today's Gaza refugee camps). Why did the Egyptians do this? According to Arafat, it was to get the Arabs out of the area because the Egyptians wanted a free hand in conquering the Negev and the southern part of the coastal plain. They wanted no interference from the locals, and no debt to them that would have to be repaid later on.[2]

THE ATTACK

By May 15, 1948, the British had evacuated their forces from all of British Mandatory Palestine. The Jews now had a free hand in defending themselves. And the Arab countries had a free hand in attacking with armies from Lebanon, Syria, Jordan, Iraq, and Egypt, along with volunteers and soldiers from Saudi Arabia, Yemen, and Morocco. Pouring into the area, these forces outnumbered the Israel Defense Forces about five to one. For the next month or so, the Israelis were involved in a desperate defensive war, barely able to keep the invaders at bay.

In June, the UN imposed a ceasefire. When the fighting resumed in July, the IDF, which had used the respite to import arms and aircraft from Russia and Germany, went on the offensive and succeeded in driving the Arab armies out of both the Jewish areas and large parts of the areas that the UN had intended to be the Arab state (Western Galilee and the southern coastal plain north of Gaza). When this offensive began, more Arabs fled.

Contrary to revisionist Arab propaganda, however, there

was never any intent to massacre Arabs, nor any efforts at what is today called ethnic cleansing. There were no reports in the world press, including the Arab press and those elements of the Western press openly hostile to Israel, about any such actions of which Israel today stands condemned. There were no such accusations from any Arab spokespersons during this time, even at the very height of the refugees' flight and for many years thereafter.

THE DIPLOMATIC RECORD

During the Rhodes armistice talks in February 1949, Israel offered to return to the Arabs the lands it had conquered that were originally meant to be part of the Palestinian state, in exchange for a peace treaty. This would have allowed hundreds of thousands of refugees to return to their homes. The Arabs said no, because, as they themselves admitted, they were on the verge of mounting a new offensive that would involve some nine thousand terrorist attacks, mostly from Egypt, over the next six years and would help ignite another war in 1956.

At the Lausanne conference in August 1949, Israel again offered to repatriate a hundred thousand refugees even without a peace treaty. The Arab states refused again because such a negotiation would have involved a tacit recognition of the State of Israel.

Instead, the Arabs insisted on maintaining the refugees in their squalor and suffering. Arab spokespersons in Syria and Egypt were quoted in their newspapers as saying that they would maintain the refugees in their camps until the flag of Palestine flew over all of the land. They would go back home only as victors, on the graves and corpses of the Jews. Moreover, as some Arabs were candid enough to announce in public, the refugee problem would serve as "a festering sore on the backside of Europe," easily converted to moral leverage in the effort to win the emotional support of the West against Israel.

CONCLUSION

The Arab refugee problem has been a heavy weight on Israel in the years since independence, the chief charge leveled against it in the court of world opinion. But while the exigencies of war certainly played a part in the creation of the refugee problem, it was primarily the handiwork of the belligerent Arab states that defied the United Nations, invaded Israel, encouraged the Arabs to flee, and then purposefully kept them in a state of wretched poverty as propaganda hostages. The problem was intentionally exacerbated by the Arab states' rejection of UN resolutions and the Geneva Conventions, their refusal (except for Jordan) to integrate any refugees into their own borders, and their refusal to enter into peace negotiations with Israel.

In his detailed *Records of Dispossession*, Michael Fischbach carefully documents Israel's offer of reparations as part of the resolution of the refugee problem.[3] At the Rhodes conference in 1949, individual refugees and whole groups tried to meet with Israeli representatives to seek reparations. But Arab leaders torpedoed such talks and prevented the "official" refugees they controlled from meeting with the Israeli delegation, thus destroying the possibility of a financial restitution for the refugees. The United States and the United Nations insisted that restitution and resettlement would be the basis of a reasonable solution to a problem that could only grow worse. But the Arab states refused this or any other possible solutions. Some Arab leaders openly expressed their lack of concern for the refugees, many of whom were clearly hostile to the Arab delegations.

Later, Israel again offered restitution and the return of frozen bank accounts and the contents of safe deposit boxes. Under pressure from Arab governments, refugees refused to fill out forms needed to verify ownership because the mere paperwork might imply recognition of Israel. So Israel rewrote the forms to placate the refugees, but only a tiny fraction ever submitted the requests.

In 1960, Israel was still trying to find ways to pay reparations to refugees via secret contact through Cypriot authorities, but Arab states intervened and shut down this option. As late as 1964, the U.S. Department of State compiled a comprehensive evaluation of refugee property, which Israel agreed to use as the basis for negotiations for just compensation. Again, the Arab states refused to negotiate, keeping the lost opportunity secret from the refugees.

6 | The Myth of Colonial Occupation

IN JUNE 1967, the opinion of the world was unanimous: Israel had been the victim of aggression in the Six-Day War, and its swift victory in the conflict was an act of self-defense. In the years since then, however, Arab mythmakers have attacked the basic facts of the war as part of their effort to recast Israel as a "fascist" presence in the Middle East, and to construct a narrative of a four-decade-long Israeli "occupation." Their propaganda has succeeded well enough to require a look back at what actually happened in 1967 and what has happened since.

"EXTERMINATION OF THE ZIONIST EXISTENCE"

In April 1967, the Soviets accused Israel in the United Nations of mounting a massive military buildup on the Syrian border. Israel denied the accusation, and the UN, under Secretary-General U Thant, sent a commission to investigate. It quickly ascertained that the Soviets were lying. There was no Israeli military massing at Syria's gates.

But there was a huge movement of Egyptian armor into the Sinai Peninsula. On May 14, Israel sent a message to Egypt at the UN: "Israel wants to make it clear to the government of Egypt that it has no aggressive intentions whatsoever against any Arab state at all." But on that same day, Nasser demanded the withdrawal of the UN peacekeeping force—established in 1957 as an international "guarantee" of safety for Israel—from the Sinai. The UN obeyed so quickly that three Egyptian army divisions and six hundred tanks had rolled into the eastern Sinai and taken up battle positions on Israel's western border by the following afternoon.

Over the next few weeks, Cairo Radio's Voice of the Arabs broadcast messages to the world: "All Egypt is now prepared to plunge into total war which will put an end to Israel"; and "As of today, there no longer exists an international emergency force to protect Israel. . . . The sole method we shall apply against Israel is a total war which will result in the extermination of Zionist existence."

On May 19, Nasser announced the blockade of the Strait of Tiran in the Red Sea, severing Israel's southern maritime link to the outside world. The next day, Syria's defense minister (later president-for-life) Hafez al-Assad said that Arab forces were ready "to explode the Zionist presence in the Arab homeland. The Syrian army, with its finger on the trigger, is united."

On May 30, Jordan's King Hussein signed a five-year mutual defense pact with Egypt and set up a joint command with Nasser, committing his country to the impending conflict. Even the Iraqis joined Nasser's military alliance against Israel, with President Rahman Aref announcing on May 31: "This is our opportunity to wipe out the ignominy which has been with us since 1948."

With the noose around it tightening, on June 5, at 4:10 A.M., Israel launched a defensive preemptive strike. Its air force fighter planes took off from bases in Israel, successfully flew across the Sinai under Egyptian radar and attacked the Egyptian air force while its planes were on the ground. With most of Egypt's air force destroyed while the pilots were still asleep, the Israeli fighter planes turned east to do the same thing to the Jordanian, Iraqi, and Syrian air forces.

After this attack had begun, the Jordan Legion initiated its bombardment of Jerusalem and Petah Tiqwa. Then Israel sent a message to King Hussein via the Romanian consulate (which had offices in both East and West Jerusalem) that was brief but unambiguous: If you stop the bombardment now, we will consider it to have been your "salvo of honor" paying lip service to the Arab world's demand for your participation. Stop the bombardment now and we will not invade the West Bank.

But King Hussein had already received a phone call from Nasser, who, although he knew that his air force was in ruins, said that Egyptian planes were over Tel Aviv and his armor was advancing on Israeli positions. Hussein believed him and disregarded Israel's plea. Had he heeded Israel's request, the West Bank and East Jerusalem would have remained under Jordanian rule. Instead, Hussein plunged into the fray, ordering his artillery to target West Jerusalem, hitting civilian locations indiscriminately and firing on the Israeli parliament building and the prime minister's office.

REJECTING PEACE

On June 19, after its swift victory, the Israel unity government declared that it was ready to return the Golan Heights to

79

David Meir-Levi

Syria, Sinai to Egypt, and most of the West Bank to Jordan, in return for peace treaties with its Arab neighbors, normalization of relations, and a guarantee of free navigation through the Strait of Tiran. Abba Eban, Israel's UN representative, made a historic speech inviting Arab states to join Israel at the peace table and informing them unequivocally that everything but Jerusalem was negotiable. He reiterated the fact that territories taken in the war could be returned in exchange for formal recognition, bilateral negotiations, and peace.[1]

Rather than accept Israel's invitation (the first time in world history that the victor had begged the vanquished for peace), eight Arab heads of state emphatically rejected this offer at an Arab summit conference in Khartoum, Sudan (August 29 to September 1, 1967), thus forcing Israel to assume control unwillingly over the nearly one million Arabs living in the West Bank and the Gaza Strip.

Despite this rebuff, the Israeli government felt that surely at least Jordan, the most reluctant member of the Arab war coalition, might cooperate and accept the return of most of the West Bank. To that end, Israel embarked on secret talks with Hussein shortly after the war. But Hussein, fearing the consequences of breaking ranks with the other Arab leaders, backed out. One man who breathed a sigh of relief at Hussein's decision was Yassir Arafat, who admitted later on in his authorized biography that if a deal had been struck between Israel and Jordan, Hussein certainly would never have permitted a Palestinian state to rise on the West Bank.[2]

The UN initially shared Israel's optimistic expectation that the Arabs would agree to a negotiated settlement. On November 22, 1967, after weeks of haggling, the Security Council put forth Resolution 242 calling for the "belligerent parties" to "work for a just and lasting peace in which every state can live in security." To that end, Israel would withdraw its forces "from territories occupied in the recent conflict," and the Arabs would affirm the right of every state in the region "to live in peace within secure and recognized boundaries free from threats or acts of force." There would be "a just settlement to the refugee problem" and a guarantee of the "territorial inviolability of every state."

Israel unconditionally accepted the resolution. The PLO and every Arab state unconditionally rejected it.[3]

SOVEREIGNTY AND ITS CONSEQUENCES

Having conquered territory in a defensive war, and having its offer to return much of that territory in exchange for peace spurned, Israel became the legal sovereign over the conquered territories. It was both necessary and completely within Israel's rights to initiate a plan of development for both Israeli and Arab residents. Sometimes referred to as "Israel's mini Marshall Plan," this initiative benefited the Arabs of the West Bank and the Gaza Strip as well as the Israelis, and it gives the lie to the idea of a heartless and illegal "occupation."[4]

From late 1967 onward, Israel invested in roads, sewage treatment plants, telephones, electricity, water, radio, sanitation, medical facilities, and other infrastructure that brought the West Bank up to twentieth-century standards. The gross domestic product of the West Bank grew at rates of between 7 percent and 13 percent per year over the next twenty-five years. Tourism brought revenue; foreign currency flowed into the shops, stores, and restaurants; infant mortality plummeted and life expectancy increased. Under the Israelis, the Palestinians had the highest standard of living of any Arab country with the exception of the oil states.

Was Israeli authority "genocidal," as claimed by Arab propagandists and their European allies, who today make insulting analogies between the Israelis and the Nazis? If so, it was the most ineffectual genocide in human history, for between 1967 and 1993 the Arab population of the West Bank and the Gaza Strip tripled, from around 950,000 to more than 3,000,000. New villages mushroomed throughout the West Bank with such rapidity that by 1993 there were some 260 new Arab towns on the map.

The bridges over the Jordan River were kept open (even though Jordan was still formally at war with Israel), and West Bank Arabs could pass freely into Jordan and elsewhere. Movement throughout the West Bank and the Gaza Strip, and between these areas and Israel, was mostly free and uninhibited. Employment was at a historic high, with West Bank and Gaza Strip Arabs working in the Israeli economy in ever-growing numbers. By 1993 there were almost 300,000 Arabs employed in Israel's tourism, agricultural, and manufacturing industries. Israelis shopped in Ramallah and Bethlehem. West Bank Arab youth came to the University of Haifa to study in the Arab studies department. Seven universities grew up in the West Bank and the Gaza Strip, where only three small teacher-training colleges had existed before.

Such facts—and the parallel fact that under the Palestinian Authority from 1994 to the present these living standards eroded precipitously, with GNP sinking to one-tenth of what it was under Israeli control—must be weighed against the international condemnation of Israel's "illegal occupation" and the decrying of its various farming and manufacturing and bedroom communities in the West Bank as "apartheid settlements."[5]

THE SETTLEMENTS

These communities or "settlements"—which are a legacy of the legal sovereignty that Israel was forced to assume over the lands it conquered in 1967—are now the core of the Arab charge that Israel is a colonialist oppressor.

There are four types of settlements on the West Bank: agrarian settlements for security purposes, manned mostly by soldiers; settlements of Jews returning to sites occupied by Jews prior to 1948 (Hebron, Gush Etzion, the Jewish Quarter of East Jerusalem); expanding suburbs of Israeli cities on or near the "Green Line"; and illegal rogue settlements.

Agrarian Settlements

Soon after the war, agrarian settlements with a military presence were established along what the Israel Defense Forces felt were crucial corridors of defense, especially along the Jordan River, near the Green Line, in the Golan Heights, and near Gaza. Because Egypt, Syria, and Jordan remained belligerent states, because the PLO was actively trying to develop bases for terrorism in the newly conquered territories, and because Israel had previously been invaded across these areas, these settlements were intended primarily to serve a strategic military defensive purpose.

In several cases where Palestinian farmers utilized the Israeli court system to lodge complaints that the army was unnecessarily taking land without proper military purpose,

David Meir-Levi

the Israeli High Court of Justice decided in favor of the plaintiffs. The army site at Beth El (near Ramallah) is the best-
known case, and probably one of the few cases in all of world
history where the legal system of the victorious country
decided in favor of the defeated, contrary to the security-
related demands of the victor's own army.

Settlements of Israelis Returning to Prior Homes

The return of civilian Israelis to homes they had owned
prior to 1948 in the West Bank began shortly after the 1967
war, with a small group setting up a few households in the
former Jewish section of Hebron, followed by a larger reset-
tling of Jews in the rapidly reconstructed Jewish Quarter of
East Jerusalem. Jews had lived in Hebron almost continuously
since the days of Joshua until the Arab pogroms of 1929,
when scores were slaughtered, hundreds wounded, and the
entire community driven from its millennia-old domicile.
Jewish habitation in Jerusalem had a similar millennia-long
history, with the 1948 war and the massacre of about half
the population of the Jewish Quarter terminating Jewish
presence there.

Later, Jews resettled the villages of the Kfar Etzion area
(A.K.A. Gush Etzion) southwest of Bethlehem. This area
had been extensively settled and developed by Zionist pio-
neers in the early part of the twentieth century, and mobs of
Arab irregulars had massacred almost half the Jews of these
villages during the 1948 war.

Settlements On or Near the Green Line

After 1967, unoccupied areas around Jerusalem and to
the east of Kfar Saba and Netania (near Tel Aviv) and to the

northeast of Petah Tiqwa were used as sites for major building projects that created low-cost housing for the expanding populations of the Jerusalem and Tel Aviv areas. In
most cases, the land utilized for these projects had been Jordanian "crown land," to which no individual could lay legal
claim of private ownership. Israel's expropriation of these
unoccupied areas flowed from its defensive actions against
an aggressor nation (Jordan) that refused to engage in peace
negotiations following the conflict.

In cases where West Bank Arabs legally owned land that
Israel wanted for these expansion projects, Israel sought to
buy the land at fair market prices. Land sale to Israel was
fairly active throughout the decades after the Six-Day War.
So much so that when the Palestinian Authority was established in 1994, Arafat declared that sale of land to Jews was
a capital offense; and as a result, Palestinian families who
had benefited from these sales were suddenly in mortal
danger and some were forced to flee the West Bank.

The rapid growth in Jerusalem's Jewish population after
the 1967 war presented the Israeli government with both a
problem and a solution of considerable political valence.
Areas of dense Jewish settlement were developed in order to
accommodate this growth, and these settlements were used
to surround Jerusalem so that the 1948–1967 phenomenon
of a "Jerusalem Corridor" (where Jerusalem was surrounded
on three and a half sides by hostile Arab towns and villages,
with access to other Israeli areas restricted to only one nar-
row road) would not be re-created in the future. The outlying
areas (French Hill, Ammunition Hill, Gilo, Ma'aleh Adumim,[6]
etc.) were turned into high-rise suburbs that expanded
the city's perimeter and accommodated the burgeoning

population. Of these, only Gilo was built on privately owned land. (A Christian family in Beit Jalla sold the hilltop site to the municipality of Jerusalem in 1974.)

Illegal Rogue Settlements

Illegal settlements were set up by breakaway settlers, often contrary to IDF and/or government instructions, sometimes on privately owned Palestinian land. Palestinian complaints about such illegal land grabs have been adjudicated in the Israeli court system, with decisions not infrequently in favor of the plaintiffs. These settlements are considered illegal by many in Israel. Some have been forcibly dismantled, despite the significant proportion of Israelis demanding that Jews be allowed to settle freely anywhere in "the Promised Land" where Abraham is thought to have lived.

Anti-settlement feeling among Israelis is spurred in large part by these rogue sites; it is almost exclusively this type of settlement on the West Bank that Prime Minister Sharon considered dismantling—even in the absence of peace negotiations with the Palestinian Authority—before illness forced him from office.

THE SETTLEMENTS AS AN OBSTACLE TO PEACE

The role of the settlements in the context of the current conflict is a complex and endlessly contentious issue precisely because Arab propaganda has been so effective in establishing as axiomatic that the settlements are: illegal, an inherent obstacle to peace, a concrete sign of Israel's intent to constitute itself as a permanent colonial enterprise occupying the West Bank and the Gaza Strip.

The Legality of the Settlements

Anti-settlement spokespersons (Arab, Israeli, and other) have repeatedly branded the settlements as illegal in accordance with the Fourth Geneva Convention and international law. But according to the Fourth Convention, the prohibition of exiling conquered populations and settling populations from the conqueror's territory into conquered territories pertains to gains resulting from an offensive war. These sections of the Convention were written to deter future actions like those of the Nazis in Eastern Europe during World War II. But since Israel acquired sovereignty over the territories in a defensive war, it is questionable whether these prohibitions apply. The fact that at least one belligerent opponent (Jordan) remained at war (until 1994) meant that the conquered population was potentially hostile for twenty-five years after the conflict.

Moreover, as we have seen, Israel never exiled any Arabs from anywhere in the territories (except in 1992 when it deported about four hundred terrorists to southern Lebanon in an attempt to stop terror activities). On the contrary, because of Israel's "open bridges" policy across the Jordan River, Arabs migrated into the area in vast numbers.

According to Eugene Rostow, one of the drafters of UN Resolution 242, the plain meaning of this resolution is that Israel's administration of the West Bank and Gaza is completely legal until a just and lasting peace is achieved. Such administration, in the absence of a peace treaty, and in the

David Meir-Levi

face of continued hostility from Arab nations and terrorist groups, can include the development of unoccupied segments to house a growing population. Such activity is not the same as transporting population to the territory for resettlement. "Rogue" settlements are plainly illegal and have been denounced as such by many Israeli politicians.

Are the Settlements an Obstacle to Peace?

From 1949 to 1967 there were no settlements in the West Bank or the Gaza Strip. Nor was there peace. The settlements to which the Arabs objected at that time were Tel Aviv, Haifa, Hadera, Afula, etc.—in other words, the settlement of Israel itself. Immediately before and immediately after the Six-Day War, and before there were any Israeli settlements in the West Bank or the Gaza Strip, Israel proposed a peace initiative that would have ended the settlements before they began. This offer was summarily refused.

In 1979, as part of the accord with Egypt, Israeli settlements in Sinai were evacuated. This showed clearly that in the context of a peace treaty, settlements are negotiable, and can be (and in fact were) dismantled. Also in 1979, as part of the accord with Egypt, Israel froze settlement expansion for three months to encourage entry of Jordan into the Egypt-Israel peace process. Jordan refused. Arafat (then engaged in creating a terrorist state in southern Lebanon) was invited to join Egypt at the peace talks, and this settlement freeze was intended to encourage his participation. He too refused.

The peace accords discussed at Madrid, Wye, Oslo, and Taba all included the acknowledgement that many, but probably not all, of the settlements will be dismantled in the context of a peace agreement. In August 2005, under the

88

"hawkish" Prime Minister Ariel Sharon, Israel decided unilaterally and unconditionally to withdraw from the Gaza Strip, forcibly removing more than nine thousand Israelis, many of whom had lived in their Gaza homes all their lives, and leaving behind tens of millions of dollars worth of factories and hi-tech hothouses for the use of the Gaza Arabs. Far from bringing peace, the destruction of these settlements encouraged Hamas and its followers to more violence, more murder, more terrorism, more war.

Do the Settlements Make Territorial Compromise Impossible?

Currently, about 250,000 Jews live in a total of 144 communities scattered through the West Bank. Eighty percent of them could be brought within Israel's pre-1967 borders with only a very minor rearranging of Green Line boundaries. Part of former prime minister Ehud Barak's offer to Arafat in 2000 at the Camp David II negotiations was the exchange of other land to compensate the Palestinians for the small number of settlements that could not be practically dismantled.

This offer was in addition to approximately 95 percent of all the disputed land in the West Bank and 100 percent of the territory in Gaza, which were to be under the control of the Palestinian Authority. Arafat rejected this offer.[7]

"Apartheid Wall"

Called by Israel a defensive barrier, the fence that Israel erected between itself and the West Bank is known by its opponents as the "apartheid" or "land grab" wall. Whatever name it is given, there is no doubt that this fence has made

Israel safer. A 2004 study by the Jerusalem Center for Public Affairs estimated that it had cut terrorist attacks by 90 percent. Ramadan Shalah, leader of the Palestinian Islamic Jihad, admitted on Al-Manar TV (Hezbollah's version of Al-Jazeera) that the fence is an all too effective impediment to his group's terror attacks: "If it weren't there, the situation would be entirely different."[8]

The Oslo Accords intentionally and specifically granted Israel the right to erect a separation fence that would afford security to Israeli communities located in pre-1967 Israel and in the West Bank and the Gaza Strip. "Israel shall continue to carry the responsibility for overall security of Israelis and Settlements, for the purpose of safeguarding their internal security and public order, and *will have all the powers to take the steps necessary to meet this responsibility.*"[9] Yassir Arafat agreed—in writing—to the premise that Israel would have the right to protect not just those Israelis within the Green Line but Israelis in general, including those in the "settlements."

Many other countries have security barriers, and some are more formidable than the provisional one Israel has constructed. Consider, just as a few examples, the fence separating Spain from Morocco at Ceuta, the British fence that ran through Belfast in Northern Ireland, the fence dividing North and South Korea, the fence that China built to keep out starving North Koreans, the fence dividing Greek from Turkish Cyprus, the fences between India and Pakistan and between India and Bangladesh, the fence between Botswana and Zimbabwe, the fence between Kyrgyzstan and Uzbekistan, the fence recently built by Saudi Arabia to stop weapons smuggling from Yemen, and of course the controversial security fence planned to extend hundreds of miles on the U.S.–Mexico border.

This latter fence in particular is intended to keep out impoverished immigrants seeking a better life for themselves and a better future for their children. Israel's defensive barrier keeps out homicidal/suicidal terrorists seeking to blow up innocent victims and make sure there is no future for Israel. What then makes Israel's fence so controversial? It comes back to the idea of an "occupation."

The Palestinians claim that the fence will gobble up a huge part of the West Bank and should have been built on what they claim to be the internationally recognized pre-1967 border between Israel and Palestine (the Green Line), if it were not a land grab in disguise. In fact, the initial route of the fence would have enclosed about 15 percent of the West Bank. The Israeli High Court of Justice ruled on several occasions in favor of Palestinian plaintiffs and forced the army to change the route of the fence to favor Palestinian demands. As a result, the modified route encompasses only around 7 percent of the West Bank.[10]

Moreover, the Green Line is an armistice line, not a border, and certainly not a legal boundary between the West Bank and Israel. There is no internationally recognized border there because the majority of the Arab world (all of the Arab world before 1979) refused to make peace, negotiate borders, and recognize those negotiated borders. Therefore, there is no legal reason to use the Green Line as a baseline or benchmark in the definition of Israel's boundaries vis-à-vis the West Bank.

Palestinians also hold that "the wall" creates a political reality adverse to a negotiated settlement. This is patently false. Because the barrier is 96 percent chain-link fence and only 4 percent concrete, even calling it a "wall" is misleading. Pretending that it is made entirely of permanent materials lends credence to the false idea that the land it has enclosed has been annexed by Israel. The barrier is a wall only in those areas where Palestinian high ground affords terrorist snipers the ability to shoot randomly into Israeli cars or living rooms, or to kill pedestrians. It is built to be removed if and when terrorism is replaced by diplomacy.[11]

But the most emotional Palestinian charge is that this is an "apartheid wall" meant to dehumanize Palestinians in the way that the government of South Africa once tortured its black population. While the term shows the cleverness of the Palestinians in appropriating highly charged metaphors, it is literally absurd. Apartheid refers to a systematic and architectonic set of laws and sanctions that allows a minority of one race to subjugate the majority of another by legal and sometimes violent means. None of this obtains in the Israeli sovereignty over the Arabs of the West Bank (or the Gaza Strip prior to 2005).

Prior to Arafat's post-Oslo terror war, there was no fence and no wall. Neither were there any checkpoints, roadblocks, curfews, or lockdowns. West Bank and Gaza Arabs shopped in Tel Aviv, and Israelis shopped in Ramallah and Bethlehem and East Jerusalem. The economy of the West Bank and the Gaza Strip was relatively prosperous, and the Arab population—which had more than tripled from 1967 to 1994—was increasingly well off. All this came to a halt only after Arafat began his terror war. The restrictions misleadingly termed "apartheid" are the result solely of Israel's need to stop the terrorism.

Does the "land grab wall" impose unreasonable hardships on the Palestinians? Certainly some suffer. Farmers are delayed in accessing some parts of their farmland. Commerce and communication across the barrier are slowed by the need for checkpoints and for the careful security searches of cars and trucks and the physical persons of pedestrians. Even ambulances are stopped and searched.

On the other hand, Israel has made extensive efforts to construct the fence in a way that will minimize hardship for the Palestinians and be as compatible as possible with the rhythms of their daily lives. But the crucial question from the Israeli point of view is: where the casualties should be and of what magnitude.

With the barrier, the casualties are the inconvenienced Palestinians.

Without the barrier, the casualties will be the scores or hundreds or thousands of Israelis who will die at the hands of terrorists who would otherwise have been stopped by the barrier.

A HISTORY OF REJECTIONISM

We saw in a previous chapter that there was no state in 1948 for the Arabs of British Mandatory Palestine, despite the best intentions of the UN and despite Israel's willingness to share the land, because the Arab leaders and the leaders of surrounding Arab nations had other plans both for the Jews, whom they intended to kill or drive out, and for the land, which they intended to annex.

David Meir-Levi

But why no state in the sixty years since? To say that there have been "missed opportunities" is not quite right because such a term suggests happenstance. In fact, the opportunities have not been missed; they have been rejected outright by the Arab world and the Palestinians. The fate of Israeli offers to the Palestinians—all based on land for peace —suggests that the Palestinian leaders and those in the surrounding Arab countries all have other plans, and these plans do not include Israel.

Since the Peel Commission's partition plan of 1937, there have been at least a dozen offers to create a state for the Palestinians on part of Israel and alongside Israel. Every offer has been accepted by Israel but rejected by the Arab world, including the leaders of the Palestinians.

The Camp David Accords

The first Camp David Accords created the peace agreement with Egypt in 1979. During the negotiations, which had stretched over five years, the Israeli prime minister, Menachem Begin, agreed to a three-month freeze on Israeli settlements in the West Bank as a confidence-building gesture, and urged the Palestinian government (Arafat, the PLO, and related factions) to join Israel and Egypt at the conference table and nullify the Palestinian National Charter's declaration of a commitment to the total dismantling of the State of Israel and the creation of a Palestinian state in its place.

Arafat rejected the invitation and refused any interaction with the Israelis. Instead, the PLO and various terrorist factions escalated terrorist activities against the civilian population of Israel from inside of Lebanon.

———

94

The Fahd Plan

This plan was formulated in 1981 at the Arab Summit Conference in Fez, when Crown Prince Fahd of Saudi Arabia proposed that the Arab states call for a unilateral declaration of a Palestinian state. This plan threw the Israeli government into turmoil because it had no ready response. But it did not matter. The Arab response was prompt and almost universal. The plan was rejected by every other participant at the Fez summit, including the PLO representative, because it would have involved a de facto recognition of the State of Israel.

The Madrid Talks

The talks held in Madrid in October 1991 raised the hopes of both Israelis and Palestinians. At the invitation of the United States and the USSR, Israeli delegates met with representatives of the leading families of the Palestinians on the West Bank and the Gaza Strip, and with Syria, Lebanon, and Jordan. PLO terrorist leaders were excluded, at Israel's request, because the PLO continued to maintain that its sole objective was the destruction of Israel.

The goal of the conference was modest: just get peace talks started, and develop the agenda at future meetings. This seemed to both Israelis and Palestinians like an ideal time for local Arab leadership on the West Bank and the Gaza Strip to step forward and take the initiative for establishing some sort of momentum toward peace.

Arab leaders, however, insisted on flying almost daily from Madrid to Tunis to receive orders from Arafat. Even though he had been utterly defeated in Lebanon in 1982 and had languished in exile for almost ten years in Tunis, his promises of victory and of the destruction of Israel still gripped the hearts and minds of enough local leaders that they would not take advantage of what the big powers regarded as a golden opportunity.

The people of Israel were willing to countenance harsh and painful compromises to achieve peace. The Palestinian leaders wanted Arafat.

The Oslo Accords

In 1993, under President Clinton's guidance, Israel agreed again to talk about the creation of an autonomous Palestinian state. A partner for peace negotiations would have to be created from the ranks of the terrorist cadres, so the PLO was given legitimacy as the Palestinian Authority (PA), and Arafat was brought out of his exile in Tunis to head the organization, which would have its capitol in Ramallah.

In exchange for agreeing to eschew terror, end incitement, disarm and dismantle the terrorist groups under his control, and settle all differences by negotiation, Arafat was given control over all Palestinians, time to build the infrastructure of a functioning state, and the opportunity to negotiate with Israel for resolution of questions relating to the creation of an independent Palestinian state. The withdrawal of Israeli military forces from the West Bank and Gaza began. The last Israeli tank left Ramallah in September 1995.

The Arab response was to betray every agreement signed at Oslo. Arafat created a police force three times the permitted size and armed it with illegal heavy weapons for offensive warfare. In addition, the PA began a media war and an education program in its primary schools which taught that Israel has no right to exist. (The maps used in geography classes did not show Israel at all.) Under this indoctrination, Israel's occupation was likened to Nazi Germany, the Holocaust was denied, and the mandate of the ultimate Palestinian state was declared to be "from the river to the sea."

Further undermining the prospects for the peace accords it had duplicitously signed, the PA, in collusion with Hamas and a dozen other terror groups, began a terror campaign against Israel. Since the first car bombing in Tel Aviv in 1994, there have been approximately 28,000 terror attacks, 1,700 Israelis killed, and more than 7,000 wounded, along with at least 6,000 Palestinians killed, unknown thousands wounded, and almost 2,000 Palestinians killed in extrajudicial murders by PA agents for the crime of "collaboration" with Israel.

Camp David II

In July 2000, Israel's Ehud Barak, working with Bill Clinton, made the most generous offer ever to the Palestinian leadership: 97 percent of the West Bank and the Gaza Strip, and a PA capitol in East Jerusalem, in return for an end to the conflict. The result? As the *New York Times* columnist Thomas Friedman noted, Israel extended the olive branch and Arafat torched it, with the second Intifada.

In an attempt to quell the escalating violence, Clinton suggested a "bridge plan" to pave the way for a return to the negotiating table. This plan was similar to Barak's, but even more generous. Arafat turned his back on this too.

Why did this last-ditch effort at a settlement fail? Some critics have contended that Barak's offers, certified by

David Meir-Levi

Clinton, were actually less generous than claimed by Israel's supporters. Proof of the opposite comes not only from Clinton, who held Arafat responsible for the breakdown of negotiations, but from an even more unimpeachable source: Prince Bandar bin Sultan, the Saudi Arabian royal ambassador to Washington. In a 2003 interview in the *New Yorker*, Ambassador bin Sultan stated that Arafat had agreed, in a phone conversation with him, that this was the "best offer imaginable." Bin Sultan went on to tell Arafat that if he took the offer, then the Saudi royal family would support him and his new state; but if he did not take the offer, it would be a crime against the Palestinian people. There would be a war, and the Saudi royal family could no longer support him.[12]

Arafat rejected the offer and the Intifada continued.

The Road Map

On September 17, 2002, representatives from the European Union, the United Nations, Russia and the United States ("The Quartet") met to form a plan that would lead to the resolution of the Arab-Israeli conflict. In October, President Bush issued a more detailed version called "The Road Map to Peace."

The Road Map envisioned a three-stage process whereby the Palestinian Authority would end terrorism and incitement of Jew-hatred (in PA schools and mosques and media), and Israel at the same time would stop settlement expansion and gradually withdraw from areas of the West Bank and Gaza.

The order of the steps is instructive: "A two state solution to the Israeli-Palestinian conflict will only be achieved through an end to violence and terrorism, when the Palestinian people have a leadership acting decisively against terror and willing and able to build a practicing democracy based on tolerance and liberty."

The "supportive measures" to which Israel agreed could not be carried out—not only because all the terrorist groups rejected the Road Map, but also because both Arafat and Mahmoud Abbas (Arafat's successor as president of the PA) declared their commitment to continuing terror activities against Israel.

Unilateral Withdrawal in Gaza

In August of 2005, under Ariel Sharon's leadership, Israel relocated nine thousand Israeli residents of the Gaza Strip, most of whom had lived and worked there for years, and destroyed (at the request of the Palestinian Authority) all seventeen Israeli communities there. This was a painful, costly, and politically very difficult step. But the Israeli government agreed to it in order to "jump-start the peace process." In addition to withdrawing its people, Israel left behind millions in high-tech infrastructure for the Palestinians' use in economic development.

In the elections that followed Prime Minister Sharon's debilitating illness, his party, now under the leadership of Ehud Olmert, won the leadership position with a substantial plurality, on a peace platform of additional territorial compromises in the West Bank in exchange for peace.

The response from Hamas and the PA was violence. More terror attacks were launched from the Gaza Strip after Israel's unilateral withdrawal than in the previous four years. Hamas declared that terror had won the concession from Israel, so terror would continue. And it did—not only

David Meir-Levi

with Hamas in Gaza but on the border with Lebanon in August 2006, when Hezbollah crossed over into Israel and attacked an IDF patrol, killing three and capturing three others and igniting the Second Lebanon War.

CONCLUSION

The last sixty years of the diplomatic record in the Middle East may be opaque in some respects, but one thing has become very clear: the Palestinian leadership and their Arab sponsors simply refuse to take yes for an answer. While the Palestinian people sink deeper into fear and squalor, their leadership plays for time, counting on growing international impatience with the conflict and the success of the "other war" they continue to wage by a clever propaganda campaign for the hearts and minds of people in Europe and the rest of the world.

The deceptive representation of Middle East history—which defines the Palestinians as the quintessential victims, unjustly oppressed and randomly terrorized, and Israel as the quintessential oppressor, disproportionately powerful and as sinister in its ends as it is brutal in its means—has rendered up for the world a new ideology, which the scholar Bat Ye'or calls "Palestinianism." This is the geographic condensation of radical Muslim values, promoting the destruction of Israel and the Jews in the same way that jihad promotes the destruction of non-Muslim religions and cultures worldwide. To justify this quasi-religious legitimization of a second fascist and genocidal war against the Jews, Palestinianism represents the history of the Middle East as Islamic history, beginning two thousand years before the creation of Islam. Rather than an original inhabitant of the region, Israel in this view is an illegal latecomer and ethnic cleanser—invading, conquering, and ravaging the Palestinian innocents who have lived in the region "from time immemorial" and who therefore have every right to employ any means necessary to pursue their just and righteous cause of liberation.

The impact that Palestinianism has had on international politics can be seen today in the strange unreality of a UN that singles out Israel for moral excoriation while ignoring the real tragedies in Tibet, Syria, Libya, Saudi Arabia, and a host of other countries. Israel has been more condemned for human rights violations by the international body than places such as Sudan (which practices slavery and the ongoing genocide of black African Christians and animists), North Korea (which uses starvation to force its people into submission to totalitarianism), and Somalia (which carries out wholesale genital mutilation of women) taken all together.

But if Palestinianism leads to obfuscation, events on the ground in the Middle East lead to clarification. The violent response to Israel's withdrawal from Gaza shows that land will never buy peace for the Jewish state. The violent and fratricidal conquest of Gaza by Hamas debunks the notion, widely proposed in the aftermath of that organization's electoral showing in 2005, that "with responsibility comes moderation." The incitements to genocide by Iran's Ahmadinejad, Hezbollah's Nasrallah, and other sponsors of the Palestinian cause strip away a generation's rhetoric about "liberation" and "national aspirations;" and situate this movement once again in the place where it began eighty years ago with the Muslim Brotherhood and its alliance with the Nazis.

David Meir-Levi

After a hard look at its history and the myths it has created to advance its agenda, it is no longer possible to deny
what the Palestinian cause has become: part of the wider
Islamofascist jihad against the West. And it is clear too that
Israel is now the frontline state in the international war on
terror.

ACKNOWLEDGMENTS

I am very grateful to my editor, Peter Collier, for his cogent critiques and astute editing, which have made my manuscript much more readable.

My deepest appreciation goes to the founder of the David Horowitz Freedom Center, David Horowitz. He has been a truly inspirational leader and has given me invaluable guidance.

I owe a great debt of gratitude as well to all who offered unstinting support for this project and expressed their confidence in my research.

But most of all, I want to thank my wife, for her enduring patience and loving support.

We all share the vision of a world in which our children and grandchildren can live free of terrorism, a goal we believe this book will help achieve.

Notes

Chapter 1: The Nazi Roots of Palestinian Nationalism and Islamic Jihad

1 Rachel Ehrenfeld and Alyssa Lappen, "The Truth about the Muslim Brotherhood Terrorism," *New Media Journal* (www.newmediajournal.us), June 17, 2006. For a critique of the term "Islamic fascism" see Eric Margolis, "The Big Lie about 'Islamic Fascism,'" at www.ericmargolis.com.

2 Abdullah Azzam, a Palestinian Muslim Brotherhood preacher, was a mentor to the al-Qaeda leader Osama bin Laden; see Zvi Mazel, "How Egypt Molded Modern Radical Islam," *Jerusalem Issue Brief*, vol. 4, no. 18 (February 16, 2005), Institute for Contemporary Affairs, at the Jerusalem Center for Public Affairs, www.jcpa.org/brief/brief004-18.htm. Mr. Mazel is the former Israeli ambassador to Egypt and to Sweden. See also Haneef James Oliver, *The Wahhabi Myth: Dispelling Prevalent Fallacies and the Fictitious Link with Bin Laden*, 2nd ed., with a summary at www.thewahhabimyth.com/ikhwan.htm.

3 Ron Leshem and Amit Cohen, "The Moslem Brotherhood," *Yediot Aharonot* (Hebrew), September 28, 2001 (posted in translation by Jonathan Silverman); and cf. also "Al-Ikhwan al-Muslimun (the Muslim Brotherhood)," at www.thewahhabimyth.com/ikhwan.htm.

4 Serge Trifkovic, "Islam's Nazi Connections," *FrontPageMagazine.com*, December 5, 2002; and cf. also Robert O. Paxton, *The Anatomy of Fascism* (Knopf, 2004). Also Martin Kramer, "Islamism and Fascism: Dare to Compare," at www.geocities.com/martinkramerorg/2006_09_20.htm.

5 Chuck Morse, "The Nazi Connection to Islamic Terrorism: Adolf Hitler and Haj Amin al-Husseini"; and also Morse's "The Nazi Origins of Modern Arab Terror," at *Morse Code*, www.chuckmorse.com/; and at *NewsMax.com*. See also Matthias Kuentzel, "National Socialism and Anti-Semitism in the Arab World," www.matthiaskuentzel.de/artikel.php?artikelID=86, July 2005.

6 Morse, supra n. 5; Kuentzel, supra n. 5; and cf. also a recent Danish

Notes

cinematic rendition of some of the photographs of Haj Amin with Khanjar and German troops: Bayerischer Rundfunk, min 5:41, at www.youtube.com/watch?v=d51poygEXYU&eurl=http%3A%2F%2Fdan sk%2Dsvensk%2Eblogspot%2Ecom%2F2006%2F08%2Fhitler%2Dmufti% 2Dof%2Djerusalem%2Dand%2Dmodern%2Ehtml.

7 As quoted in Kuentzel, "National Socialism and Anti-Semitism in the Arab World" (supra n. 5).

8 Ibid. Eichmann's lieutenant, Dieter Wisliceny, at his own trial for war crimes after World War II, agreed that the following was a proper description of Haj Amin al-Husseini: "The Mufti is a sworn enemy of the Jews and has always fought for the idea of annihilating the Jews. He sticks to this idea always, also in his talks with [Adolf] Eichmann. . . . The Mufti is one of the originators of the systematic destruction of European Jewry by the Germans, and he has become a permanent colleague, partner and adviser to Eichmann . . . in the implementation of this programme." See Transcript of the Trial of Adolf Eichmann, Session 50, published by The Nizkor Project, www.nizkor.org/hweb/people/e/eichmann-adolf/ transcripts/Sessions/Session-050-07.html.

9 Thomas Krumenacker, "Nazis Planned Holocaust for Palestine: Historians," Reuters, April 7, 2006, a review of a recent study by two Holocaust scholars.

10 For a summary of Qutb's life and influences, see Paul Berman, "The Philosopher of Islamic Terror," *New York Times Magazine*, March 23, 2003, www.nytimes.com/2003/03/23/magazine/23GURU.html.

11 A voluminous bibliography detailing the Qur'anic and post-Qur'anic literature of Jew-hatred can be found at www.oclc.org/support/documentation/firstsearch/databases/dbdetails/details/ATLAReligion.htm.

Chapter 2: *The Communist Face of the Palestinian National Movement*

1 Ion Mihai Pacepa, *Red Horizons* (1987); and cf. also Pacepa's "The Story of Creation," *Wall Street Journal*, September 30, 2004.

2 In 1972, for instance, a large load of Soviet and Eastern bloc weaponry was sent by Fatah to the IRA but was seized in Antwerp. In 1973, a five-ton shipment of Soviet and East German weapons sent from Libya to the IRA was captured in Ireland. In 1977, a load of Soviet weapons from the

PLO in Lebanon—consisting of assault rifles, submachine guns, rocket launchers, hand grenades and explosives—was seized, again at Antwerp; and in 1979, a similar cache of Soviet-manufactured weaponry was captured in Athens.

3 Christopher Story, "An Extensive Expose of International Terrorism," www.thefinalphase.com, September–October 2001; and cf. "Soviet Analyst: Soviet Terrorism Unmasked," www.freerepublic.com/focus/news/689872/posts; and cf. also J. Michael Waller, "International Terrorism: The Communist Connection Revisited," Institute of World Politics, Papers and Studies, June 1, 2002.

The PLO is composed of several different, and sometimes competing, terror groups. The Popular Front for the Liberation of Palestine (PFLP) is the more radical, more Marxist-Leninist, less Islamic partner of Fatah. It has generally taken a hard line on Palestinian national aspirations, opposing the more moderate stance of Fatah. It opposed the Oslo Accords and was for a long time opposed to the idea of a two-state solution to the Israeli-Palestinian conflict, but in 1999 came to an agreement with the PLO leadership regarding negotiations with Israel.

4 The following is based upon Martin Gilbert, *Israel: A History* (William Morrow, 1998); Alan Hart, *Arafat: Terrorist or Peace Maker?* authorized biography (London, 1984); Peter Mansfield, *A History of the Middle East* (Penguin, 2002); Conor Cruise O'Brien, *The Siege: The Saga of Israel and Zionism* (Simon & Schuster, 1986); Ion Mihai Pacepa, *Red Horizons*; Barry M. Rubin & Judith Colp Rubin, *Yasir Arafat: A Political Biography* (Oxford University Press, 2003); and Howard Sachar, *A History of Israel: From the Rise of Zionism to Our Time* (Knopf, 1996).

5 Arlene Kushner, "Abu Mazen: Beneath the Moderate Veneer," *FrontPageMagazine.com*, February 25, 2005.

6 Efraim Karsh, "Arafat's Grand Strategy," *Middle East Quarterly*, Spring 2004.

7 Abu Iyad (A.K.A. Salakh Halaf), *My Home, My Land: A Narrative of the Palestinian Struggle*, autobiography, trans. Eric Roudeau (Times Books, 1981).

8 Ibid.; and J. R. Nyquist, "Kremlin Puppets and How They Work," *WorldNetDaily* (www.worldnetdaily.com), October 19, 2000.

9 Pacepa, *Red Horizons*, passim.

10 Nyquist, "Kremlin Puppets and How They Work" (supra n. 7).

Notes

11 Ibid.; and Joel S. Fishman, "Ten Years Since Oslo: The PLO's 'People's War' Strategy and Israel's Inadequate Response," Jerusalem Center for Public Affairs, September 15, 2003, www.jcpa.org/jl/vp503.htm.

12 Rashid Khalidi, *Palestinian Identity: The Construction of Modern National Consciousness* (Columbia University Press, 1997). See also Philip Hitti, *History of the Arabs*; and for conflicting analysis compare George Antonius, *The Arab Awakening: The Story of the Arab National Movement*; and also B. Kimmerling and J. Migdal, *The Palestinian People*.

13 James Dorsey, "Wij zijn alleen Palestijn om politieke redden," *Trouw*, March 31, 1977.

14 Alan Hart, *Arafat: Terrorist or Peace Maker?*

15 Yossef Bodansky, "Arafat's 'Peace Process,'" Ariel Center for Policy Research, Policy Paper #18, 1997, www.acpr.org.il/publications/policy-papers/pp018-xs.html; and cf. also Abu Iyad, *My Home, My Land* (supra n. 6).

Chapter 3: Islamofascism

1 Ar-Risala, September 13, 2001, quoted in MEMRI, Special Dispatch Series no. 268, September 17, 2001, www.memri.org/bin/articles.cgi?Area=jihad&ID=SP26801.

2 Adrian Morgan, "Hamas, Gaza, and the Muslim Brotherhood's 'Project,'" Family Security Foundation, July 10, 2007, www.familysecurity matters.org/index.php?id=1132779, and Daniel Goldhagen, "A Manifesto for Murder," *Los Angeles Times*, February 5, 2006; and cf. also the Intelligence and Terrorism Information Center, at the Center for Special Studies, Jerusalem, for various publications with general information and history on Hamas and its terrorist leaders.

3 For translations of Muslim historians who exult in Islam's 1,300 years of transcontinental carnage and sword-point conversions, see Andrew G. Bostom, *The Legacy of Jihad: Islamic Holy War and the Fate of Non-Muslims* (Prometheus Books, 2005). For a modern summary of the bloody and almost genocidal history of Islamic jihad, read the arabophile Sir John Bagott Glubb's *The Great Arab Conquest*, and *The Great Arab Empires*.

4 See the "Hamas Covenant, 1988" (August 18, 1988), at the Avalon Project, Yale Law School, www.yale.edu/lawweb/avalon/mideast/hamas.htm.

5 The discussion of Hamas leadership is developed in more detail in

David Meir-Levi, "Hamas über Alles," *FrontPageMagazine.com*, February 24, 2006.

6 ADL, "Recent Attacks against Israel," www.adl.org, January 24, 2006; and cf. also IMRA, www.imra.org.il, January 8, 2004.

7 Note that following the Six-Day War, when Israel decided not to annex the West Bank and the Gaza Strip in the hope that it would soon return these territories to Jordan and Egypt in the context of peace treaties, Jordanian law was officially maintained, and government and social service institutions, including many charity organizations, were allowed to continue their operations. Some of these charity organizations were Hamas fronts, such as the Committee for Aid to Orphans and Prisoners and the Islamic Aid Society.

8 This and much of the following text is compiled from information available through CAMERA (www.camera.org), MEMRI (www.MEMRI.org), PMW.org, and Israeli government websites.

9 Nathan Brown, *Palestinian Politics*, passim; in his footnotes he gives a number of examples of this ploy, used by both Arafat and Hamas.

10 Amira Howeidy, "What Truce?" *Al-Ahram Weekly Online* (Cairo), no. 623, January 30–February 5, 2003, at http://weekly.ahram.org.eg/2003/623/eg4.htm.

11 Yehudit Barsky, "The New Leadership of Hamas: A Profile of Khalid al-Mish'al," American Jewish Committee, May 2004; and cf. also Ryan Jones, "Terrorist Nominated as New PA Prime Minister" Jerusalem News Wire, February 20, 2006; and "The 'Pragmatist' of Hamas," at *Honest Reporting* (www.honestreporting.com), February 19, 2006.

Chapter 4: Zionists Stole Our Land

1 As a barely tolerated minority under Islam, the Jews of the Holy Land fell into the category of "dhimmi": noncitizen residents denied basic human rights and tolerated only at the whim of the local Muslim ruler. Dhimmi Christians and Jews in Israel suffered the depredations and discrimination that were characteristic of the plight of dhimmi throughout most of the Muslim world and across most of Muslim history. The Jews of the Holy Land, as we know not from Turkish history but from the reports of Christian travelers, suffered two horrific pogroms under the Turks: one 1834 in Hebron; and one in 1836, when Arab mobs rioted

Notes

against the Jews of Saffed (Tzfat) for thirty-three days, unchecked by Turkish police, killing hundreds of Jews, destroying homes and shops, raping and murdering. Cf. Bat Ye'or in *The Myth of Islamic Tolerance: How Islamic Law Treats Non-Muslims*, ed. Robert Spencer (2005), pp. 137ff.

2 For an objective presentation of the documentation, see Justin McCarthy, *The Population of Palestine: Population History and Statistics of the Late Ottoman Period* (Columbia University Press, 1990).

3 The above discussion relies heavily upon the work of Alexander Scholch, Gershon Shafir, and Neville Mandel (see bibliography).

4 The above discussion relies heavily upon the work of Shmuel Almog, Arieh Avneri, Mitchell G. Bard, Michael R. Fischbach, Martin Gilbert, and Conor Cruise O'Brien (see bibliography).

5 Most of the following summary is drawn from David Fromkin, *A Peace to End All Peace*; Martin Gilbert, *Israel: A History*; Efraim and Inari Karsh, *Empires of the Sand*; McCarthy, *The Population of Palestine*; and Howard Sachar, *A History of Israel: From the Rise of Zionism to Our Time*.

6 Horace B. Samuel, *Unholy Memories of the Holy Land* (London, 1930).

7 For this period see Gilbert, *Israel: A History*; Conor Cruise O'Brien, *The Siege: The Saga of Israel and Zionism*; Sachar, *A History of Israel*; and Shoshanna Harris Sankowsky, *A Short History of Zionism*.

8 When it became clear that the British Mandate was soon to end, Jewish leadership prepared for war. Already organized with a shadow government in the form of the Jewish Agency for Palestine, the Jews possessed the infrastructure to mobilize forces and make political and military decisions. Clandestine weapons purchases, recruitment and training of troops to the Haganah forces, and planning for defensive campaigns were all undertaken in secret, while political activism in the West was stepped up.

The Arabs of Palestine possessed no such organization. Their leaders, lacking any national identity or governmental infrastructure, looked to the surrounding Arab states for guidance and support. As Yassir Arafat noted, Palestinian Arabs at that time had no sense of national identity and no political organization beyond local clans and effendis. Thus, while sporadic but deadly terrorist attacks against Jews were carried out, there was no overarching strategy, nor was there any unity among the leadership. See Alan Hart, *Arafat: Terrorist or Peace Maker?* for references to Arafat's admission that the Arabs of Mandatory Palestine had no national identity.

9 The most famous of these Arab targets was the village of Deir Yassin. Arab propaganda accuses the Israelis paramilitary force of perpetrating a massacre there. However, here as elsewhere, history proves the Arab propaganda wrong. (See pp. 70ff. for a detailed discussion of Deir Yassin.) The PBS documentary *The 50 Years War* indicates that an Iraqi force had entered the village in order to use it as a base against Jerusalem. Thus it was a legitimate target for military action. Moreover, Yassir Arafat notes in his authorized biography (Alan Hart, *Arafat: Terrorist or Peace Maker?*) that the Egyptians used the Deir Yassin "massacre" to terrorize the Palestinians of the south, so that they could be more easily herded into makeshift concentration camps in the Gaza area. The Egyptians forcibly disarmed the Arabs of southern Palestine and killed those who tried to escape from the camps. Arafat unequivocally blames the Egyptians for the problem of Arab refugees from southern Palestine who ended up in the refugee camps of the Gaza Strip. See Hart for Arafat's anecdotal testimony to these Egyptian war crimes.

10 Gilbert, *Israel: A History*.

Chapter 5: The Political Abuse of the Refugee Issue

1 During a 1998 lecture at Shechem's An-Najah University, senior Fatah Central Committee member Sakher Habash said: "To us, the refugee issue is the winning card which means the end of the Israeli state."

2 Conor Cruise O'Brien, in *The Siege: The Saga of Israel and Zionism*, offers perhaps the most objective summary of the facts supporting these conclusions. See also Alan Hart, *Arafat: Terrorist or Peace Maker?* for Arafat's accusation against Egypt.

3 Michael R. Fischbach, *Records of Dispossession: Palestinian Refugee Property and the Arab-Israeli Conflict*, The Institute for Palestine Studies Series (Columbia University Press, 2003).

Chapter 6: The Myth of Colonial Occupation

1 For documentation of the sequence of events in Jerusalem, cf. www.sixdaywar.co.uk/timeline.htm; www.sixdaywar.co.uk/news_articles-life-on-the-seam.htm; and www.sixdaywar.co.uk/gloria-report-jerusalem-compared.htm.

Notes

Recently published material from Soviet archives supports the assertion that the USSR was integral in prompting the Arabs to start the war; because Russia was sure that the Arabs would win, and in doing so, the Arab armies would destroy Israel's nascent nuclear reactor in Dimona. Cf. Gideon Remez and Isabella Ginor, *Foxbats over Dimona: The Soviets' Nuclear Gamble in the Six-Day War* (Yale University Press, 2007).

2 Alan Hart, *Arafat: Terrorist or Peace Maker?*

3 For the Khartoum conference, where the Arab rejection of Israel's peace offers was officially formulated, and the infamous "three Khartoum NO's" cf. www.mideastweb.org/khartoum.htm.

4 Information summarized above about international law regarding land acquired through aggression vs. land acquired through defensive actions is drawn from Eugene Rostow, "Historical Approach to the Issue of Legality of Jewish Settlement Activity," *New Republic*, April 23, 1990; Rostow, "Are the Settlements Legal? Resolved." *New Republic*, October 21, 1991; Stephen Schwebel, "What Weight to Conquest," *American Journal of International Law*, vol. 64 (1970); and Julius Stone, *International Law and the Arab-Israel Conflict*, extracts from Israel and Palestine-Assault on the Law of Nations, ed. Ian Lacey. 2nd ed. (2003), www.aijac.org.au/resources/reports/international_law.pdf.

5 The above account is based upon economic reports from the World Bank and from UN evaluations of the economic status of Arab states and the Palestinian Authority territories in 2003, 2004, and 2005. See also Milan Kubic, "The West Bank Today," *Newsweek*, June 13, 1977, p. 55. For a summary of West Bank and Gaza Strip economies under Israel, cf. Efraim Karsh, "What Occupied Territories?" *Commentary*, July 2002. For the UN reports, see United Nations Development Programme (UNDP), *Arab Human Development Report 2002* (July 2, 2002). The report, compiled by a group of distinguished Arab intellectuals, is available at www.undp.org/arabstates/ahdr2002.shtml. For the most recent UN study, with additional commentary on the prosperity of the West Bank and the Gaza Strip under Israeli sovereignty, cf. UN Development Programme, *Arab Human Development Report 2005* (September 7, 2005), at www.undp.org/arabstates/ahdr/2005.shtml.

6 In a recent controversial announcement, the Israeli self-described human rights organization B'Tzelem declared that at least 40 percent of

the land used for the construction of high-rise apartments in Ma'aleh Adumim, a bedroom community east of Jerusalem, was land that had belonged to individual Arab owners (i.e., not crown land). When forced to open its maps and calculations to public scrutiny, B'Tzelem could demonstrate only about 0.5 percent of Ma'aleh Adumim's land which was privately owned by Arabs. And cf. "IDF Refutes Land Claim," *Jerusalem Post*, March 4, 2007. B'Tzelem lied. See www.jnewswire.com/article/1789; and also the Associated Press in *International Herald Tribune*, March 14, 2007.

7 The failure of Camp David II was due in large part to Arafat's strategy of pocketing Barak's concessions, making no substantive concessions in return, and then demanding more from Barak. See Dennis Ross, *The Missing Peace* (2005); William Clinton, *My Life* (2006); Elsa Walsh, "The Prince," *New Yorker*, March 24, 2003, p. 49ff., for details of Arafat's tactics of rejection, recrimination, and mendacity.

8 *JCPA Middle East Briefing*, vol. 7, no. 8 (July 7, 2004); and cf. also www.mfa.gov.il; www.israelfm.org/publicaffairs/catalog.htm; and www.securityfence.mod.gov.il/Pages/ENG/default.htm. And cf. also Intelligence and Terrorism Information Center, at the Center for Special Studies, Jerusalem, November 15, 2006, reporting on Shalah's interview on Al Jazeera dated November 11, 2006. More recently, none other than Musa Abu Marzuq, deputy chair of the Hamas political bureau, bemoaned the fact that Israel's defensive barrier has made suicide bombings more difficult. Cf. Intelligence and Terrorism Information Center, June 7, 2007, www.terrorisminfo.org.il/malam_multimedia/English/eng_n/html/hamas_060607e.htm. For a summary of the barrier's effectiveness from a professional source, cf. "Is Israel Winning? Statistics Tell a Surprising Story," *Jane's Foreign Report*, www.foreignreport.com, July 14, 2004.

9 Ruth Wedgwood, "Professor Ruth Wedgwood Analyzes the Security Fence Case at the World Court," exclusive journalists' briefing, *Access Middle East*, January 28, 2004, "The World Court Case on Israel's Security Fence: Legal and Political Implications."

10 D. Makovsky and A. Hartman, "Israel's Newly Approved Security Fence Route: Geography and Demography," Washington Institute for Near East Policy, *PeaceWatch*, no. 495, March 3, 2005, and cf. www.washingtoninstitute.org/mapImages/4228b0b09c392.pdf; and www.washingtoninstitute.org/templateC05.php?CID=2268; and cf. also www.tinyurl.com/2u9hl for more on this issue.

Notes

11 For historical perspective cf. Irshad Manji, "How I Learned to Love the Wall," *New York Times*, March 18, 2006. Ms. Manji is a Canadian Muslim journalist who openly critiques the many irrational and immoral anti-Israel positions of the Arab world, including the endless mendacious diatribe against Israel's defensive barrier.

12 Elsa Walsh, "The Prince," (supra n. 7).

Bibliography

General Background

Alon, Yigal. *The Making of Israel's Army.*

Almog, Shmuel. *Zionism and the Arabs: Essays.*

Antonius, George. *The Arab Awakening: The Story of the Arab National Movement.*

Asher, Jerry, and Eric Hammel. *Duel for the Golan: The 100-Hour Battle That Saved Israel.*

Avneri, Arieh. *The Claim of Dispossession: Jewish Land Settlement and the Arabs, 1878–1948.*

Bard, Mitchell G. *The Complete Idiot's Guide to Middle East Conflict.*

———. *Myths and Facts: A Guide to the Arab-Israeli Conflict.* Available at www.jewishvirtuallibrary.org/source/myths2/mftoc.html

Bat Yeor. *The Dhimmi: Jews and Christians under Islam.*

———. *Eurabia: The Euro-Arab Axis.*

———. *Islam and Dhimmitude: Where Civilizations Collide.*

Blum, Howard. *The Eve of Destruction: The Untold Story of the Yom Kippur War.*

Bodansky, Yossef. *The High Cost of Peace: How Washington's Middle East Policy Left America Vulnerable to Terrorism.*

Bostom, Andrew. *The Legacy of Jihad: Islamic Holy War and the Fate of Non-Mislims.*

Boyne, Walter U. *The Yom Kippur War and the Airlift That Saved Israel.*

Brackman, Nichole, and Asaf Romirowsky. "Dubious Refugee Relief," *Washington Times*, June 21, 2007; also at www.meforum.org/article/1706

Braude, Joseph. "Islam in the Crucible," *Playboy*, October 2006.

Brown, Nathan J. *Palestinian Politics after the Oslo Accords: Resuming Arab Palestine.*

Bibliography

Carmi, Joseph, and Arie Carmi. *The War of Western Europe Against Israel.*

Cherkashin, Victor, and Gregory Feifer. *Spy Handler: Memoir of a KGB Officer.*

Chessler, Phyllis. *The Death of Feminism: What's Next in the Struggle for Women's Freedom.*

Chomsky, Noam. *Fateful Triangle: The United States, Israel and the Palestinians.* 1999.

Clinton, William. *My Life.*

Cohn-Sherbok, Dan, and Dawoud el-Alami. *The Palestine-Israel Conflict: A Beginner's Guide.*

DeMause, Lloyd, *The Emotional Life of Nations.*

Dershowitz, Alan. *The Case for Israel.*

———. *The Case for Peace: How the Arab-Israeli Conflict Can Be Resolved.*

———. *Why Terrorism Works.*

Ehrenfeld, Rachel. *Evil Money: Encounters Along the Money Trail.*

———. *Funding Evil: How Terrorism Is Financed—and How to Stop It.*

Encyclopædia Judaica. "Israel: History."

Esposito, John. *Islam: The Straight Path.*

Finkelstein, Norman. *Image and Reality of the Israel-Palestine Conflict.*

Fischbach, Michael R. *Records of Dispossession: Palestinian Refugee Property and the Arab-Israeli Conflict.*

Friedman, Thomas L. *From Beirut to Jerusalem.*

Fromkin, David. *A Peace to End All Peace: The Fall of the Ottoman Empire and the Creation of the Modern Middle East.*

Gilbert, Martin. *The Arab-Israeli Conflict: Its History in Maps.* 1977.

———. *Israel: A History.*

———. *The Routledge Atlas of the Arab-Israeli Conflict.* 2002

Glubb, John Bagot. *The Great Arab Conquests.*

———. *The Great Arab Empires.*

———. *A Soldier with the Arabs.*

Gold, Dore. *Hatred's Kingdom: How Saudi Arabia Supports the New Global Terrorism.*

————. *Tower of Babble: How the United Nations Has Fueled Global Chaos.*

Goldberg, Bernard. *Bia:. How the Media Distort the News.*

Goodwin, Jan. *Price of Honor: Muslim Women Lift the Veil of Silence on the Islamic World.*

Gottheil, Fred. "Arab Immigration into Palestine," *Middle East Quarterly*, vol. 10, no. 1 (Winter 2003).

Gutmann, Stephanie. *The Other War: Israelis, Palestinians and the Struggle for Media Supremacy.*

Hamady, Sania. *Temperament and Character of the Arabs.* 1960.

Harari, Haim. *A View from the Eye of the Storm: Terror and Reason in the Middle East.* 2005.

Harkabi, Yehoshafat. *The Palestinian Covenant and Its Meaning.* 1979.

Hart, Alan. *Arafat: Terrorist or Peace Maker?* Authorized biography.

Hitti, Philip. *History of the Arabs.*

Hazony, Yoram. *The Jewish State: The Struggle for Israel's Soul.*

Iyad, Abu (A.K.A. Salakh Halaf). *My Home My Land: A Narrative of the Palestinian Struggle.* Translated by Eric Rouleau.

Kanaana, Sharif. *Reinterpreting Deir Yassin.* Bir Zeit University. April 1998.

Kanaana, Sharif, and Nihad Zitawi. *Deir Yassin.* Monograph no. 4, Destroyed Palestinian Villages Documentation Project (Documentation Center of Bir Zeit University, 1987).

Karetzky, Stephen, and Peter Goldman, editors. *The Media's War Against Israel.*

Karsh, Efraim. "Arafat's Grand Strategy," *Middle East Quarterly*, Spring 2004.

————. *Fabricating Israeli History: The "New Historians."* Cass Series— Israeli History, Politics, and Society. 1997.

————. *Islamic Imperialism: A History.* 2006.

Karsh, Efraim, and Inari Karsh. *Empires of the Sand: The Struggle for Mastery in the Middle East, 1789–1923.* 1999.

Katz, Samuel. *Battleground: Fact and Fantasy in Palestine.*

Khalidi, Rashid. *Palestinian Identity: The Construction of Modern National Consciousness.* 1997.

Bibliography

Kimmerling, Baruch, and Joel S. Migdal. *The Palestinian People: A History.*

Kohn, Bob. *Journalistic Fraud: How the New York Times Distorts the News and Why It Can No Longer Be Trusted.* 2003.

Kramer, Elliot. *Complicity: Terrorism in the News.*

Kushner, Arlene. *UNRWA (The United Nations Relief and Works Agency for Palestine Refugees in the Near East): A Hard Look at an Agency in Trouble.* Center for Near East Policy Research. September 2005.

Laqueur, Walter, and Barry Rubin, editors. *The Israel-Arab Reader: A Documentary History of the Middle East Conflict.*

Levins, Hoag. *Arab Reach: The Secret War Against Israel.*

Lewis, Bernard. *The Crisis of Islam: Holy War and Unholy Terror.*

———. *Islam and the West.*

———. *The Middle East: A Brief History of the Last 2,000 Years.*

———. *The Muslim Discovery of Europe.*

———. *Semites and Anti-Semites: An Inquiry into Conflict and Prejudice.*

———. *What Went Wrong? Western Impact and Middle Eastern Response.*

Livingstone, Neil C., and David Halevy. *Inside the PLO: Covert Units, Secret Funds, and the War Against Israel and the United States.*

Loftus, John, and Mark Aarons. *The Secret War Against the Jews.*

MacLeod, Scott. "Inside Saudi Arabia," *Time,* October 15, 2001.

Malley, Rob, and Hussein Agha. "Camp David: The Tragedy of Errors," *New York Review of Books,* August 9, 2001.

Mandel, Neville. *The Arabs and Zionism before World War I.*

Mansur, Salim. "Sadat's Death Was a Prelude," *Toronto Sun,* October 9, 2006. Also at *Front Page Magazine* (www.frontpagemag.com), October 9, 2006.

McCarthy, Justin. *The Population of Palestine: Population History and Statistics of the Late Ottoman Period.*

Meir-Levi, David. *Big Lies: Demolishing the Myths of the Propaganda War Against Israel.* 2005.

———. *History of the Arab-Israel Conflict.* Series in the *Jewish Community News* of San Jose, California, 2003–2004.

———. "Islamikaze War and Palestinian Poverty," *Front Page Magazine* (www.frontpagemag.com), September 15, 2004.

Bibliography

———. "Left Wing Monsters: Arafat." *Front Page Magazine*, September 23, 2005.

———. "The Missing Peace Is Missing Pieces," *Front Page Magazine*, November 24, 2004.

———. "Occupation and Settlement," *Front Page Magazine*, June 24, 2005.

———. "Terrorism: The Root Causes," *Front Page Magazine*, November 9, 2005.

Morse, Chuck. *The Nazi Connection to Islamic Terrorism: Adolf Hitler and Haj Amin al-Husseini*. 2006.

Mowbray, Joel. *Dangerous Diplomacy: How the State Department Threatens America's Security*.

Murawiec, Laurent. *Princes of Darkness: The Saudi Assault on the West*.

Netanyahu, Benjamin. *A Durable Peace: Israel and Its Place among the Nations*. 2000.

———. *Fighting Terrorism: How Democracies Can Defeat Domestic and International Terrorists*. 2001.

———. *Terrorism: How the West Can Win*. 1986.

Nydell, Margaret K. *Understanding Arabs: A Guide for Modern Times*.

O'Brien, Conor Cruise. *The Siege: The Saga of Israel and Zionism*.

Oren, Michael B. *Six Days of War: June 1967 and the Making of the Modern Middle East*.

Pacepa, Ion Mihai. *Red Horizons*.

Pappe, Ilan. *The Making of the Arab-Israeli Conflict, 1947–1951*.

Patai, Raphael. *The Arab Mind*.

PBS. *The 50 Years War: Israel and the Arabs*. DVD, 1993, 2000.

Peters, Joan. *From Time Immemorial: The Origins of the Arab-Jewish Conflict over Palestine*.

Pryce-Jones, David. *The Closed Circle: An Interpretation of the Arabs*.

Pipes, Daniel. *Militant Islam Reaches America*.

Rabinovich, Abraham. *The Yom Kippur War: The Epic Encounter That Transformed the Middle East*.

Rees, Matt. "Torn Apart," *Time*, June 18, 2001.

———. "The Enemy Within," *Time*, August 27, 2001.

Bibliography

Rogan, Eugene L., and Avi Shlaim, editors. *The War for Palestine: Rewriting the History of 1948.*

Ross, Dennis, *The Missing Peace: The Inside Story of the Fight for Middle East Peace.* 2004.

Rubin, Barry M., and Judith Colp Rubin. "The Father of Modern Terror." Interview by Jamie Glazov, *Front Page Magazine* (www.frontpagemag.com), April 4, 2005.

———. *Yasir Arafat: A Political Biography.*

Rubinstein, Danny. *The People of Nowhere: The Palestinian Vision of Home.*

Saadawi, Nawal El. *The Hidden Face of Eve: Women in the Arab World.*

———. *The Nawal El Saadawi Reader.*

Sachar, Howard Morley. *A History of Israel: From the Rise of Zionism to Our Time.* 1996.

Said, Edward W. *The Edward Said Reader.* Edited by Moustafa Bayoumi and Andrew Rubin.

———. *The End of the Peace Process: Oslo and After.* 2001.

Sankowsky, Shoshanna Harris. *A Short History of Zionism.* 1947.

Sasson, Jean P. *Princess: A True Story of Life Behind the Veil in Saudi Arabia.*

Schoenberg. Harris O. *A Mandate for Terror: The United Nations and the PLO.*

Scholch, Alexander. *Palestine in Transformation, 1856–1882: Studies in Social, Economic and Political Development.*

Segev, Tom. *One Palestine, Complete: Jews and Arabs Under the British Mandate.*

Shafir, Gershon. *Land, Labour, and the Origins of the Israeli-Palestinian Conflict: 1881–1914.*

Shapira, Anita. *Land and Power: The Zionist Resort to Force, 1881–1948.*

Sharansky, Natan. *The Case for Democracy: The Power of Freedom to Overcome Tyranny and Terror.*

Shavit, Avi. "The General," *New Yorker*, January 23, 2006.

Shlaim, Avi. *The Iron Wall: Israel and the Arab World.*

Smith, Charles D. *Palestine and the Arab-Israeli Conflict.*

Spiegel, Steven L. *The Other Arab-Israeli Conflict: Making America's Middle East Policy, from Truman to Reagan.*

Stein, Kenneth W. *The Land Question in Palestine, 1917–1939.*

Sufian, Sandra. "Mapping the Marsh: Malaria and the Sharing of Medical Knowledge in Mandatory Palestine," *Newsletter of the Palestinian American Research Center*, Spring 2002..

United Nations Development Programme. *Arab Human Development Report 2002.* Available at www.undp.org/arabstates/ahdr2002.shtml

United Nations Development Programme. *Arab Human Development Report 2004.* Available at www.undp.org/arabstates/ahdr2004.shtml

United Nations Development Programme. *Arab Human Development Report 2005.* Available at www.undp.org/arabstates/ahdr2005.shtml

Victor, Barbara. *Army of Roses: Inside the World of Palestinian Women Suicide Bombers.*

Walsh, Elsa. "The Prince," *New Yorker*, March 24, 2003.

Williams, Colleen Madonna Flood. *Yasir Arafat.* Major World Leaders series.

Ziff, William Bernard. *The Rape of Palestine.* 1938.

International Law

Rostow, Eugene W. "Are the Settlements Legal? Resolved." *New Republic*, October 21, 1991.

———. "Historical Approach to the Issue of Legality of Jewish Settlement Activity," *New Republic*, April 23, 1990.

Schwebel, Stephen. "What Weight to Conquest," *American Journal of International Law*, vol. 64, no. 2 (April 1970).

Stone, Julius. *International Law and the Arab-Israel Conflict.* Extracts from *Israel and Palestine—Assault on the Law of Nations*, edited by Ian Lacey. 2nd edition, with additional material and commentary, 2003. www.aijac.org.au/resources/reports/international_law.pdf

Arab Attitudes toward Jews

"ADL Urges U.S. Intervention to Stop Anti-Semitic Program from Airing in Egypt," Anti-Defamation League press release, October 24, 2002, www.adl.org/presrele/ASInt_13/4184_13.asp

Bibliography

"*Mein Kampf* in East Jerusalem and the Palestinian Authority," *Jewish Virtual Library*, www.jewishvirtuallibrary.org/source/anti-semitism/mein.html

Simon Wiesenthal Center, press releases concerning "blood libel" in Syria, October 21 and October 23, 2002, at www.wiesenthal.com/

Timmerman, Kenneth R. *Preachers of Hate: Islam and the War on America.*

Wistrich, Robert S. *Muslim Anti-Semitism: A Clear and Present Danger.* American Jewish Committee, 2002.

Dhimmi Status and Jews under Muslim Rule

Bat Ye'or. *The Dhimmi: Jews and Christians under Islam.* Translated from French by David Maisel, Paul Fenton, and David Littman. 1988.

Lewis, Bernard. *The Jews of Islam.* 1990.

Rubin, Ur, and David J. Wasserstein, editors. *Dhimmis and Others: Jews and Christians and the World of Classical Islam.* Israel Oriental Studies, vol. 17. 1997.

Stillman, Norman A. *The Jews of Arab Lands: A History and Source Book.* Jewish Publication Society, 1990.

Jewish Refugees

Levin, Itamar. *Locked Doors: The Seizure of Jewish Property in Arab Countries.* Translated by Rachel Neiman. 2001.

Shulewitz, Malka Hillel, editor. *The Forgotten Millions: The Modern Jewish Exodus from Arab Lands.* 2000.

Stillman, Norman A. *The Jews of Arab Lands in Modern Times.* Jewish Publication Society, 1991.

Anti-Semitism

Chesler, Phyllis. *The New Anti-Semitism: The Current Crisis and What We Must Do About It.*

Shoenfeld, Gabriel. *The Return of Anti-Semitism.*

Additional Websites Used as Reference

Beyond Images: Engaging in Israel's Battle of Information and Ideas, http://beyondimages.info/

Coalition for Responsible Peace in the Middle East, www.c4rpme.org/

Conceptwizard info, www.conceptwizard.com/info.html

DEBKAfile, www.debka.com/

Free Muslims Coalition, www.freemuslims.org/

IMRA: Independent Media Review Analysis, www.imra.org.il/

International Press Center, Palestinian National Authority State Information Service, www.ipc.gov.ps/

Jewish Virtual Library, www.jewishvirtuallibrary.org/

MEMRI: Middle East Research Institute, www.memri.org/

Palestine Facts, www.palestinefacts.org/

Palestinian Media Watch, www.pmw.org.il/

Terrorism Knowledge Base, www.tkb.org/

Index

Index

Index

Intifada (Second), 97–98

Iran, xiii, 45

Iraq, viii; creation of, 58; and Deir Yassin, 71–72; expels Jews, 62; petroleum in, 57; PLO in, 28; pro-Nazi coup in, 10; and Six-Day War, 78–79; in War of 1948, 12, 63–64, 73

Irgun, 63, 71

Irish Republican Army, 104

Islamic Aid Society, 107

Israel Defense Forces (IDF): and Hamas–PA link, 46; Jordan raid, 23–24; and settlements, 83; in War of 1948, 73; and Yassin, 43

Jazeera, Al, 50

Jerusalem, 54; Hamas in, 42, 48; as international city, 62; massacres in, 8, 60, 64, 68; as non-negotiable, 80

Jerusalem Center for Public Affairs, 90

Jerusalem Corridor, 85

Jewish Agency for Palestine, 61, 108

Jibril, Akhmed, 42

jihad, 100–2; and Arafat, 36–38; and al-Banna, 5–7; and Hamas, 43, 49; and Qutb, 16

Jihad, Abu, 28

Jordan, viii; Arafat in, 23–27; creation of (Transjordan), 12, 56, 58; expels Jews, 58–59; and Madrid talks, 95; and Muslim Brotherhood, 18; and peace talks, 88; and refugees, 75; and Six-Day War, 78–79, 82, 85, 87;

in War of 1948, 12, 63, 73, 83; West Bank annexation, xii, 19, 65; West Bank sovereignty, 23, 80, 107

Jordan Legion, 23, 26, 79

Kfar Etzion. *See* Gush Etzion

Khalidi, Hussein, 72

Knesset, 65

Kuwait, 26

League of Nations, 58

Lebanon, 58; against Arafat, 26–27; Arafat (PLO) in, 22, 24–25, 27–28, 94; expels Jews, 62; Hezbollah war in, 100; and Madrid talks, 95; and Muslim Brotherhood, 18; War of 1948, 12, 63–64, 68, 73

Lehi (Fighters for the Freedom of Israel), 60, 63

Libya, 26, 101

Madrid talks, 88, 95–96

Mao Zedong, 28

Marxism: and al-Banna, 5; of PFLP, 105; and PLO, 22, 31, 38; *see also* communism

Marzuq, Musa Abu, 42

Mash'al, Khaled, 42, 48, 49

Mein Kampf, 7

Milestones in the Road (Qutb), 16

Morocco, 12, 63, 73

Muhammad: siege of Mecca, 64

Muhse'in, Zahir, 33–34

Muslim Brotherhood, vii, 4–7; Arab wariness of, 18–20; genocidal ideology, xiii, 17; and Hamas, 4, 36, 38–39, 40, 41–

Index

refugees (*cont.*)
19, 73, 109; resettlement & restitution, 74, 75–76
refugees (Jewish), 58–62
"Road Map to Peace," 98–99
Rogers, William, 25
Roman Empire, 32; Temple destruction, 53
Romania, 20–21, 29–31, 41
Rostow, Eugene, 87
Russia, 98; pogroms in, 54; *see also* Soviet Union

Sadat, Anwar, 60
Said, Edward, 12
Said, Nuri, 69
Saudi Arabia, viii, 101; against Arafat, 26–27; Hamas funding, 45; and Muslim Brotherhood, 18; origins of, 58; Wahhabism in, 14; in War of 1948, 12, 63, 73
security barrier, 89–93; as "apartheid wall," 92–93; comparisons, 90–91; court challenges to, 91; effectiveness of, 90; and Oslo Accords, 90
"settlements," 83–89; and court challenges, 83–84, 85; legality of, 87–88; rogue, 86; security purposes, 83–85; in Sinai, 88
Shalah, Ramadan, 90
Shari'a, 9, 40, 49
Sharon, Ariel, viii, 86, 89, 99
Shukairy, Ahmad, 20, 24
Sinai, 20, 77–80, 88
Six-Day War (1967), vii–viii, x, 22, 32, 77–79; aftermath, 79–81; and Dimona nuclear reactor, 110; Khartoum conference, 21,

23; and "occupation," xii–xiii; and PLO Charter, 33; resettlement after, 84–86, 88; and USSR, 77, 109–110
Slovakia, 41
Somalia, 101
South Africa, 92
Soviet Union (USSR), ix, x; and Afghanistan, 36; and Arafat, 24, 27–28, 38; KGB & "liberation fronts," 20–22, 28, 29, 31; and Madrid talks, 95; and Six-Day War, 77, 109–110; weapons shipments, 104–5
Spain, 41
Stürmer, Der, 7
Sudan, 26, 101
Supreme Muslim Council of Palestine, 7, 8
Syria, viii, 83, 101; and Arafat (PLO), 24, 26; creation of, 58; expels Jews, 62; and Hamas, 45; and Madrid talks, 95; and Muslim Brotherhood, 18; Palestine as province of, 32; in Six-Day War, 77–80; in War of 1948, 12, 63–64, 68, 69, 70, 73

Taba peace talks, 88
Transjordan, 56, 58–59; *see also* Jordan
Turkey, 28; in World War I, 57–58
Turks. *See* Ottoman Empire

United Nations: double standard in, 101; partition (Security Council Resolution 181), vii, viii, xi–xii, 11–12, 53, 61–62, 64, 65, 66; on refugee issue, 66,

HISTORY UPSIDE DOWN has been set in Adobe Systems' Warnock Pro, an OpenType font designed in 1997 by Robert Slimbach. Named for John Warnock, one of Adobe's co-founders, the roman was originally intended for its namesake's personal use, but was later developed into a comprehensive family of types. Although the type is based firmly in Slimbach's calligraphic work, the completed family makes abundant use of the refinements attainable via digitization. With its range of optical sizes, Warnock Pro is elegant in display settings, warm and readable at text sizes – a classical design with contemporary adaptability.

SERIES DESIGN BY CARL W. SCARBROUGH